The Role of Female Seminaries on the Road to Social Justice for Women

The Role of Female Seminaries on the Road to Social Justice for Women

Kristen Welch
and
Abraham Ruelas

Foreword by
Susie C. Stanley

WIPF & STOCK · Eugene, Oregon

THE ROLE OF FEMALE SEMINARIES ON THE ROAD
TO SOCIAL JUSTICE FOR WOMEN

Wipf and Stock
An Imprint of Wipf and Stock Publishers
199 W. 8th Ave., Suite 3
Eugene, OR 97401

www.wipfandstock.com

ISBN 13: 978-1-62032-563-6

Manufactured in the U.S.A.   01/09/2015

To our fellow Christians who work with each other in a spirit of unity to promote and to defend equality for women.

"Be completely humble and gentle; be patient, bearing with one another in love. Make every effort to keep the unity of the Spirit through the bond of peace. There is one body and one Spirit—just as you were called to one hope when you were called—one Lord, one faith, one baptism; one God and Father of all, who is over all and through all and in all."

EPHESIANS 4:2–4, NIV

Dr. Kristen Welch is an Instructor of English at Cochise College in Sierra Vista, Arizona. Her publications include *"Women with the Good News": The Rhetorical Heritage of Pentecostal Holiness Women Preachers* (Centre for Pentecostal Theology Press, 2010) and *Deep Roots: Defining the Sacred Through the Voices of Pentecostal Women Preachers* (CreateSpace, 2014).

Abraham Ruelas is Dean of Academics and Professor of Communication and Psychology at Patten University and author of *"Women and the Landscape of American Higher Education: Wesleyan Holiness and Pentecostal Founders"* (Wipf and Stock, 2010) and *"No Room for Doubt: The Life and Ministry of Bebe Patten"* (Seymour Press, 2012).

Contents

Foreword

ONE AFTERNOON A STUDENT excitedly rushed into my office to tell me she had uncovered information on women attending a seminary in the nineteenth century. She mistakenly equated the meaning of the term "seminary" in that earlier time with its current reference to a school offering graduate education to people preparing for ministry. I hated to undermine her potential discovery but felt an obligation to provide an appropriate definition. What she had actually discovered was a reference to a school offering secondary education to girls. Abraham Ruelas and Kristen Welch focus on this type of seminary. They examine the history of education in the United States to tease out information relating to female seminaries, their antecedents and the institutions that later traced their roots to them. They demonstrate the role of female education, particularly in seminaries which were popular in the nineteenth and early twentieth century. Their focus illustrates social justice for women as it relates specifically to the increasing acceptance of women's equality in a society as a result of access to additional education.

Welch and Ruelas pursue an inclusive approach to their subject. They do not start with an exploration of British roots as others have often mistakenly done. They correctly begin their investigation on the West Coast during the sixteenth century among Spanish settlements. Along with a comprehensive geographical perspective, they examine education provided for Native American and African American girls as well as Caucasians. They trace the expansion of education for girls from private tutors in the home to finishing schools, from academies to seminaries and additional steps along the way. A number of female seminaries ultimately changed into colleges restricted to women. Gradually, more colleges and universities traditionally open only to men began admitting women. This slow progression in academic opportunities has contributed toward the empowerment of women enabling them to assert their equality.

While the book primarily illumines the positive role of education in girls' lives, the authors do not overlook evidence that illustrates a negative impact as well. For instance, the goal of education at the Spanish mission schools was conversion, not only to Christianity but to Spanish civilization. The degree of emphasis on cultural assimilation depended upon which religious orders sponsored the schools. The education of Native American girls more consistently illustrates an adverse effect since a primary goal was to promote assimilation by erasing the language and culture of the students. Education did not always contribute to positive results for girls. While the authors' intention is to demonstrate the positive effects of education girls in terms of increased recognition of equality, they do not ignore the negative implications when they were present. Likewise, the involvement of Christianity in female education has not always led to beneficial results. Most Christians promoted assimilation in the mission schools and in schools for Native Americans which they sponsored. Today, this objective is placed on the negative side of the ledger. Ruelas and Welch acknowledge this history.

This text, however, provides a strong corrective to studies that overlook or deny the significant positive role of Christianity in both establishing and promoting girls' education. To a large extent, education for girls in this country can be traced to Christian origins. They accurately identify Christianity as being responsible for advances in educational opportunities for girls. For instance, the Ursuline Sisters founded the first female academy in what became the United States in 1727 followed closely by the creation of a Moravian school in Pennsylvania. In the nineteenth century, Christian groups began establishing seminaries which particularly contributed toward fostering women's equality.

This work covers the big picture by examining changes in curriculum that demonstrate opportunities for females to receive additional education. During the eighteenth century, daughters of wealthy families studied primarily ornamental subjects which included topics such as dancing and drawing. Gradually, useful subjects joined ornamental subjects, expanding the curriculum to include classes that were more academically focused. Slowly, the balance shifted from ornamental to useful subjects. While the lines between the two were often blurred, over time the balance shifted from ornamental to useful subjects.

As seminaries replaced earlier forms of education for girls, curriculum offerings began to more closely resemble that of boys' schools. The authors supplemented their overview with in depth pictures of curriculum provided by individual schools, sometimes retrieved from archival sources. For example, the text includes an examination of curriculum at well-known schools such as Mary Lyon's Mt. Holyoke Female Seminary as well as lesser known schools such as Farmville Female Seminary.

Education opportunities improved dramatically when associated with cultural expectations for women. This was often unintentional as the explicit goal of these ideologies was to train women to better fulfill their place as mothers within the home. But education tended to subvert this agenda, ultimately propelling women toward further equality. The concept of Republican Motherhood offers an excellent example. Again, a quick definition is in order. The use of "republican" in this phrase is not to be confused with the current political party. The term was coined to describe the prescribed role of mothers in the early decades following the founding of the United States. The concern was to raise sons to foster the political ideals of the new republic. Mothers were encouraged to exert their political influence in the home rather than in the political arena. There was no place for women in the public arena of politics. Their involvement in nation-building was solely behind the scenes in the private realm of the home. Obviously, this social construct supported a highly restrictive role for women. However, it played a dramatic part in furthering women's education in order to prepare them for this important task. Unintentionally, it provided a stepping stone in that increased education ultimately led to women's involvement in all areas of public life.

The notion of woman's sphere became another popular societal construct by mid-nineteenth century and remnants of it pop up periodically to this day. Woman's sphere revolved around her domestic role, again seeking to limit her activities and influence to the home. Proponents of woman's sphere grounded their case in their interpretation of Scripture, going so far as to argue that God ordained a separate sphere for women with clear boundaries. Promoting idealized roles in the home led to the call for further education to train girls to be better wives and mothers. Catherine Beecher is a notable example of an educator who shared this goal. Her agenda was conservative but resulted in positive gains for women because she fostered education. Increased educational opportunities unwittingly contributed to women's equality which undermined her original objective. Education extended women's place, subverting attempts to limit women's involvement in the public arena. Others appropriated woman's sphere, not by arguing against the idea but by seeking to expand that sphere. They established normal schools which trained women as public school teachers. Promoting women as teachers eventually resulted in teaching being acknowledged as an acceptable occupation for women. Education extended women's place by subverting attempts to limit women's involvement in the public arena.

Following the Civil War, African Americans promoted another cultural conviction, the Talented Tenth. Initially composed of the top African American men in the country, the Talented Tenth would be educated to facilitate the transition to middle and upper class status, both economically and socially eventually benefitting all African Americans. Advocates of education for African American girls soon included women in the equation to justify expanding their chances for learning. Spelman College, founded as Atlanta Baptist Female Seminary before the term "Talented Tenth" was coined, furthered the agenda of establishing women's place in the Talented Tenth.

It is hard to imagine our foremothers being denied even a minimal education, for whatever reason. No one would employ arguments today (at least not publically!) that rely on the claim that girls have reduced mental capacity which results in an inability to learn. Now, we take co-educational opportunities at every academic level for granted. Ruelas and Welch have documented the long road to achieving this reality.

Susie C. Stanley

Professor of Historical Theology,
Messiah College (1995–2011)
Founder and Executive Director,
Wesleyan/Holiness Women Clergy, Intl. (1991-2006)

Preface

ONE OF MY FAVORITE poems is by N. Scott Momaday. It is called "The Delight Song of Tsoai-talee."[1] In it, Momaday uses repetition to express how he feels about being in love by using natural imagery. Two examples are: "I am a feather on the bright sky / I am the blue horse that runs in the plain." As an English professor, I like to read through this poem with my students and ask them to explain what it means. The looks on their faces as they piece together the fluidity of the speaker's metaphoric expressions of joy and as they begin to notice his use of anaphora to capture the rhythm and to build energy never gets old. After discussing the poem, I ask them for three metaphors about themselves to describe who they are and how they feel. It is one of my favorite assignments.

In the same way, I am tempted to offer my own metaphors about women who experienced feelings about education that were just as great and as overwhelming as Momaday's speaker in the poem. These women were desperate to receive an education –they were women like me who were born with a burning desire to ask questions and to seek their answers using the best resources available and learning from the best teachers they could find. However, unlike Momaday, I imagine over worn metaphors like mountains to be climbed and oceans to be sailed and paths to be cleared and battles to be fought. These dry comparisons just won't do.

So instead of offering clumsy attempts at poetry, I want to offer you insights into the minds of those women who pushed hardest for the education of their fellow sisters by drawing on primary texts that express metaphors

---

1. Momaday, "The Delight Song of Tsoai-talee."

like going "from butterflies to eagles"[2] to show the effects of education on women. In this book, Dr. Ruelas and I draw on primary and secondary texts to show that the remarkable American women of the eighteenth, nineteenth, and early twentieth centuries did not simply argue for *any* education, but for a proper education. They argued for an *equal* education. They argued for women to enter into the teaching sphere, perhaps knowing that allowing women to become the experts in this profession would effectively and forever destroy the arguments of opponents to women's education who claimed women were not intellectually capable of absorbing the same concepts and of performing the same intellectual tasks as men. As teachers, they would absorb knowledge and, subsequently, its power.

To achieve goals like these, Emma Willard protested the desires of young women for an education that produced objects like paintings and needlework, not knowledge like math and rhetoric by offering us these metaphors: "If they [educators] attend chiefly to the cultivation of the mind, their work may not be manifest at the first glance; but let the pupil return home, laden with fashionable toys, and her young companions, filled with envy and astonishment, are never satisfied till they are permitted to share the precious instruction."[3] With ornamental education reduced to "fashionable toys" and the mind elevated to a garden to cultivate, she made clear her goals. She wanted her audience, the New York legislature, to help her establish a seminary that would help her students and their parents understand what an education could be and why it was so valuable.

In this same argument, Willard bravely confronted her detractors in society by rejecting a lack of precedence for educating women as a valid excuse for inaction. Combining her zeal for equal educational opportunities for women with her passion for the United States, she offers us the personification of history (she "lifts not her finger"), a new metaphor of "shackles" to tie to unwanted "authority and precedent," and she ends with the personification of our country with men and women joined to protect "her" (i.e., "to defend her," "to protect her," "to raise her") in this excerpt:

> Yet though history lifts not her finger to such an one, anticipation does. She points to a nation, which, having thrown off the shackles of authority and precedent, shrinks not from schemes of improvement, because other nations have never attempted them; but which, in its pride of independence, would rather lead than follow, in the

2. Horowitz, *Alma Mater*, 329.
3. Willard, "An Address to the Public," 10.

march of human improvement: a nation, wise and magnanimous to plan, enterprising to undertake, and rich in resources to execute. Does not every American exult that this country is his own? And who knows how great and good a race of men, may yet arise from the forming hand of mothers, enlightened by the bounty of that beloved country,—to defend her liberties,—to plan her future improvement,—and to raise her to unparalleled glory?[4]

Catharine Beecher also cleverly turned housewifery into a science, which was a metaphor strategically designed in order to raise the status of women's work. With a book co-authored by her famous sister Harriet called *Principles of Domestic Science: as Applied to the Duties and Pleasures of Home, a Text-book for the Use of Young Ladies in Schools, Seminaries, and Colleges* (1871), she elevated the work of women. Additionally, her considerable influence on propelling women into the teaching profession was based on a commonly used metaphor of her time: Mothers were melded into politicians and preachers, shaping the political and religious views of children from their birth. Likewise, teachers were "mothers" of the nation's children, guiding their political (and religious) views in the classroom. These metaphors were effective arguments and were essential for justifying an education for women that went beyond ornamental topics.

Willard, Beecher, and many others set the stage for equality in education. Yet the story of how education was shaped is not a simple one of battles being won decisively with using just the right arguments. While the hotbed of education has been in the northern states with women in those states having a literacy rate about four times higher there than in the south as of 1860, women gained access to education in all kinds of ways throughout the country in the eighteenth, nineteenth, and twentiethcenturies.[5] Yet access was not equal. Not all women had the basic skills they needed to engage in higher-level studies, nor did they all have access to seminaries or academies because of economic and regional disadvantages. Social constructs in the South were very different from those in the North, particularly within larger cities, and some were not as quick to embrace education as others were. Life in the West for whites, African-Americans, and Native Americans was a different experience than it was for others during the nineteenth century and the volatility of their existence provided unique challenges for them that obstructed access to education for many.

4. Ibid., 34–35.

5. Eisenmann, *Historical Dictionary*, 375.

Even with all of these differences, there are common themes in the story Dr. Ruelas and I have to tell.

One chapter of this book offers a list of about 135 female seminaries and academies opened across the United States and other chapters explore Mexican, British, Italian, and American roots that led to the right for women to be educated. One chapter shares excerpts from a centennial celebration at the Cherokee Female Seminary that challenges our ideas about Native American history and another illustrates the heartbreaking obstacles African-American women had to overcome by using a metaphor from within their community called "The Talented Tenth." These chapters repeat some of the same components of history as contexts are laid out for the reader, but in ways that reveal the relevance of that history to the story being told in a particular chapter.

For Americans interested in reading a history that has not been watered down, glossed over, and reduced to abstractions in order to appeal to a busy reader, the primary texts we draw upon balance these tendencies, although any history will be reductive in places in the interest of time and limitations on length. By putting Christianity back into its central role in American history, the stories and artifacts left to us are proof that while some twisted Christian principles to excuse monstrosities like slavery and the cultural annihilation of Native Americans (misusing rhetoric as St. Augustine once warned in his fourth-century defense of rhetoric in *De Doctrina Christiana*) others have sought out truth and faith and used their persuasive words to correct the course of history. In short, the recovery of these primary texts is a gift to readers interested in a much more nuanced narrative of women's history than we have received in recent years. It is a complicated history, but one that should shape feminist scholarship in the future.

To close, the idea for this book was born out of a simple desire to answer questions that were inspired by a historical marker on Longwood University's campus (formally Farmville Female Seminary). On it were grainy photos of women in long dresses with ruffled fronts. Perched on their heads were large, fancy hats. As someone who has studied and published on the subject of women preachers, I was intrigued by the word "seminary." I wanted to learn more about these women. While they did not attend the seminary to become preachers, they were part of the many Christians who helped make room for women to enter into any field, including the ministry, for those who came after them.

As I sketched out my ideas for a book on this topic, I decided I didn't want to embark on this alone. Having read Dr. Ruelas' book (published in 2010), *Women and the Landscape of American Higher Education: Wesleyan Holiness and Pentecostal Founders*, I decided to present him with a rough outline of my ideas at a Society for Pentecostal Studies Conference based on his clear expertise in this area. Taking my ideas, he transformed them into a brilliantly worded table of contents which would serve as our outline, then took the lead in drafting a proposal, and then secured a publisher. Upon acceptance, we divided up the chapters and began the process of writing this book in 2012.

As I now write these final words at the end of two years of research, writing, and endless revisions, I am incredibly happy to close out this chapter of my life. During the two years of research and writing, the recession took my husband's job and he relocated from Virginia to Arizona to work on a contract basis until a more permanent option opened up. After he received a permanent offer of employment in Arizona, I reluctantly gave up my position as an Assistant Professor of English at Longwood University and moved out of our beautiful home. I had spent five years in that position, building a career, and traded it for two years of part-time work here in Arizona, commuting from Sierra Vista to Tucson to Douglas to teach classes as an adjunct. In the process of my long job search, we lost our home in Virginia, unable to sell it. I know our story is a common one, but is also an uncommon one because I believe God has been in control of it all. As I enter a new full-time position this fall at Cochise College right here in Sierra Vista, I know just how incredibly lucky I am. Entering back into the workforce to enjoy a regular salary and a "one-campus" teaching position is something I might have taken for granted in Virginia, but will be grateful for each and every day in my new home here in the Sonoran Desert. Finishing this book at this particular time feels like I'm closing out a very difficult chapter in my life.

I am ready to use what's left of the summer to enter into rest. Wendell Berry once wrote that when the world was too much for him, he went out to be restored by nature, to "come into the peace of wild things / who do not tax their lives with forethought / or grief."[6] Like Berry, I want to "come into the presence of still water," perhaps because the twenty-third Psalm is so ingrained in me my hope is to experience God's rest in that silent place, to feel His "goodness and mercy" follow me there. And, if you will allow

6. Berry, "The Peace of Wild Things," 102.

me one final metaphor, before the summer dies away I want to echo these words written by James Wright after an encounter with a pair of "Indian ponies": "Suddenly I realize / That if I stepped out of my body I would break / Into blossom."[7] Indeed, after exercising the benefits of an education that I will be forever grateful for, it is time to just be thankful and to rest.

I leave you with the verse God gave me when this all began:

But blessed in the [wo]man who trust in the Lord, whose confidence is in him. She will be like a tree planted by the water that sends out its roots by the stream. It does not fear when heat comes; its leaves are always green. It has no worries in a year of drought and never fails to bear fruit.

JEREMIAH 17: 7-8, *NIV*

Dr. Kristen Welch

7. Wright, "A Blessing," 69.

Acknowledgments

I WOULD LIKE TO thank Abe Ruelas who was wonderful to work with over the length of this project. Also, I would like to acknowledge the support of my husband, Jerry Welch, who has consistently cheered me on over the last twenty-one years. I would also like to acknowledge the support of my parents. In particular, I am grateful for the trip I took with my mother this spring to tour the Cherokee Heritage Center at Park Hill where the remains of the old Cherokee Female Seminary still stand and then to visit the beautiful campus of Northeastern State University in Tahlequah to see the rebuilt Seminary Hall. I would like to thank my children for allowing me to have the time to embark on my writing projects. Finally, I would like to thank the librarians at Longwood University and the University of Arizona who helped me to find much of the information that I needed in order to write this book. God bless each one of you!

Kristen Welch

First of all, I want to express my deepest appreciation to Kristen Welch for asking me to join her on the journey of writing this book. It is equally important to acknowledge my three mentors, Dr. Kimberly Alexander, Dr. Estrelda Alexander, and Dr. Susie Stanley. Each has been a wonderful influence in developing my research and writing on gender and Christianity.

Within the sphere of family I want to thank my wife Patricia for her prayers, support, and patience throughout this project. I also want to thank my mother, Rev. Teresa Ruelas, for her example as a dedicated woman of faith, her lifelong service in the field of Christian education and her prayer and financial support of this book project.

I'd like to also acknowledge Jie Howard who assisted with preparation of some of the text, Dr. Yashica Crawford for her suggestions regarding the chapter on African American seminaries and to Janice Braun, Associate Library Director and Special Collections Librarian at Mills College for her assistance with my research on the early years of the Young Ladies' Seminary, the school that became Mills College.

Abe Ruelas

1

Antecedents of the Female Seminary and the Age of Reform: "I Study Because I Must"

Spanish Roots

THE HISTORY OF OBTAINING an equal education for American women demonstrates the complexity of our progress towards social justice. For example, before the settlement of Jamestown and Plymouth, the Spanish colonized Florida and much of the Southwest.[1] The *Historical Dictionary of Women's Education in the United States* marks the education of Hispanic American women from the colonial period up to the Treaty of Guadalupe Hidalgo in 1848 that resulted in the surrender of a great deal of land.[2] Education was usually obtained in Catholic mission schools of the sixteenth and seventeenth centuries, with priests serving as teachers. They were designed to convert the "Indians" and to "spread the Catholic faith." While instruction was for boys and focused largely on trades like "masonry, hide tanning, and wine making," instruction for girls was domestic. However, Catholic women had the option to go much further with their education if they entered the convent as a nun. But not all Catholic women. Women of mixed or Indian blood were not welcome in the cloister, and women of the lower economic classes were not able to get in since admittance required a large dowry.[3]

---

1. Eisenmann, *Historical Dictionary*, 89.

2. Ibid., 202.

3. Ibid., 89.

Nuns needed higher "intellectual training" and could devote themselves to reading, reflection, and writing. Their "poems, songs, plays, and theological treatises" were largely confined to the cloister, but Sor Juana Ines de la Cruz, who lived from 1648 to 1695, became popular in the local communities, although according to a short biography of her life, she lived in Mexico and was driven to silence by the church because of a letter published by a jealous priest detailing a critique on the sermon of a Jesuit that she had voiced in a private conversation.[4] The critique of de la Cruz was used as evidence that she did not know her place within her patriarchal society and brought her under heavy criticism. The fact that the Catholic church went to great lengths to silence her and to demand that she renounce her life as an intellectual is evidence of her level of influence.

It is instructive to look at her letter in some detail to see how she couched her defense of education for women. In response to the spiteful bishop of Puebla who published her critique of the Jesuit's sermon in 1690 under the pseudonym Sister Filotea de la Cruz, Sor Juana Ines de la Cruz defended the education of women in "La Respuesta de la poetisa a la muy illustre Sor Filotea de la Cruz," or "The Poet's Answer to the Most Illustrious Sister Filotea de la Cruz," published in 1691. Her letter began with this statement: "I study because I must. I believe for the same reason that the fault is none of mine. Yet withal, I live always so wary of myself that neither in this thing nor in anything else do I trust my own judgment."[5] In this statement, she played a role made famous by Queen Elizabeth (although it is unknown if she was aware of it), by asserting her intelligence while humbly encapsulating it within self-deprecation. She then listed biblical women, just as the English Quaker Margaret Fell Fox did in her famous tract "Women's Speaking, Proved, Justified and Allowed of by the Scriptures" in 1666 to argue that women should not be silent.[6] In order to

4. de la Cruz, "From The Poet's Answer," 781–82.

5. Ibid., 784.

6. In many cases such as this one, women would structure arguments for equality in similar terms as their contemporaries or predecessors without ever being aware of the fact that someone else had already done so or at least without acknowledging their contemporaries and predecessors. Benjamin Rush, an American, drew on the same themes many women did in "Thoughts Upon Female Education" to justify the education of women:

The influence of female education would be still more extensive and useful in domestic life. The obligations of gentlemen to qualify themselves by knowledge and industry to discharge the duties of benevolence would be increased by marriage; and the patriot—the hero—and the legislator would find the sweetest reward of their toils in the approbation

demonstrate examples of women that held places in society that were out of the norm, she offered Deborah, who was "issuing laws, military as well as political, and governing the people among whom there were so many learned men," the Queen of Sheba who dared to question King Solomon, prophetesses such as Abigail, and those gifted in persuasion, such as Esther. In her long list of "the Gentiles," she included "Minerva, daughter of great Jupiter and mistress of all the wisdom in Athens, adored as goddess of the sciences," Aspasia, "who taught philosophy and rhetoric and was the teacher of the philosopher Pericles,"[7] and many others. "For what were they all but learned women, who were considered, celebrated, and indeed venerated as such in Antiquity?" she asked.

She went on to write, "And seeking no more examples far from home, I see my own most holy mother Paula, learned in the Hebrew, Greek, and Latin tongues and most expert in the interpretation of scriptures." By pointing this out, she was refuting the bishop's accusation that she was entering a masculine realm when critiquing a sermon. She went on to show how her mother was well educated and well praised, and then pointed to Proba Falconia, "a Roman woman, wrote an elegant book of centos, joining together verses from Virgil, on the mysteries of our Holy Faith." She went on to point out that Queen Isabella (Spain), the Queen of Sweden, the Duchess of Aveyro, and the Countess of Villaumbrosa were also well educated.[8]

Like so many before her, de la Cruz took on Paul in the Scriptures and used the interpretations of Dr. Arce to defend her claim that while she accepted the biblical injunction that women should not speak publicly, most

---

and applause of their wives. Children would discover the marks of maternal prudence and wisdom in every station of life, for it has been remarked that there have been few great or good men who have not been blessed with wife and prudent mothers. Cyrus was taught to revere the gods by his mother Mandane; Samuel was devoted to his prophetic office before he was born by his mother Hannah; Constantine was rescued from paganism by his mother Constantia; and Edward the Sixth inherited those great and excellent qualities which made him the delight of the age in which he lived from his mother, Lady Jane Seymour. Many other instances might be mentioned, if necessary, from ancient and modern history, to establish the truth of this proposition.

7. Pericles, as it is well known, was one of the most effective leaders of Athens, a brilliant orator, and author of a speech adapted from Aspasia, known as "The Funeral Oration" which honored the fallen in war, but also reiterated the values that bound them together culturally and politically. Aspasia's version of this oration is recorded in Plato's *Menexenus*.

8. de la Cruz, "From The Poet's Answer," 784–85.

certainly could do so privately.[9] She wrote: "Clearly, of course, he does not mean by this that all women should do so, but only those whom God may have seen fit to endow with special virtue and prudence, and who are very mature and erudite and possess the necessary talents and requirements." She went on to argue that not all men should be educated either, particularly those who are evil. "To such men, I repeat, study does harm, because it is like putting a sword in the hands of a madman: though the sword be of the noblest of instruments for defense, in his hands it becomes his own death and that of many others."

Her defense of women's education began by turning to St. Jerome and to the Scriptures and can be summed up with a request to allow women to educate their daughters instead of risk their reputations by "familiarity with men."[10] She asks: "For what impropriety can there be if an older women, learned in letters and holy conversation and customs, should have in her charge the education of young maids?" Using several examples, she showed how Scriptures and poetry can't be interpreted correctly without the historical and cultural knowledge required to contextualize them, and thus how women must be educated beyond just basic skills to fully engage with Scripture.[11] She was wise in arguing this since society widely supported allowing women to attain basic literacy in order to read Scripture and to become better Christian wives and mothers. This was a common theme in the New England colonies as well. De la Cruz advocated for private study, and justified her request that women not be silenced with her most powerful examples yet, namely those women the church has allowed to write: "Gertrude," "Teresa," and "Brigid, nun of Agreda."[12] She ended with reiterating that she should be allowed to "teach by writing," and that she did not intend to enter into theological discourse by the letter the bishop had published.[13] Indeed, if there was a biblical precedence, then it is almost impossible to argue that women should not be allowed to learn.

Although she was an example of what Mexican women could achieve, and although she offered an erudite argument for women to be educated, women's education did not progress in a positive direction for Mexican-Americans for centuries due to the effects of racial prejudice within the

9. Ibid., 785.

10. Ibid., 786.

11. Ibid., 787–88.

12. Ibid., 788.

13. Ibid., , 788.

United States. In the late nineteenth century many wealthy Mexican girls in the United States attended the Ursuline Convent in San Antonio or the Incarnate Word of Brownsville, but by 1856, they implemented a "separate but equal" law in Southwestern states that paralleled those in place for African Americans.[14] In addition, much like the Native Americans, they were punished for speaking in Spanish and were expected to fully assimilate to white culture. Very little research currently exists to pull all of the details together, but the details we do have reveal surprising parallels with the education of Native Americans.[15] Therefore, while de la Cruz provides an important antecedent, she remains an example of the enormous challenges in place for women who wished to be educated despite gender or race.

Italian and British Roots

Naturally, arguments for the education of women in the United States have British (and one notable Italian) antecedents and not all of them can be covered here. Yet it is worth mentioning a few of the best known. For example, we can look as far back as the fifteen century at the Italian Catholic Christine de Pizan (1364–1430) who argued for women's education. In *The Book of the City of Ladies* (1405), de Pizan relates a dialogue between herself and "Worldly Prudence" who was a character "meant to indicate that the book will focus primarily on the active life of a woman engaged in familial and civic affairs, rather than that of one withdrawn into the contemplative life of religion."[16] This character offered two examples of women who were educated and who successfully spoke publicly.[17] "Thus," de Pizan has Worldly Prudence say, "not all men (and especially the wisest) share the opinion that it is bad for women to be educated. But it is very true that many foolish men have claimed this because it displeased them that women knew more than they did."[18]

The British Quaker Margaret Fell (1614–1702) argued for women's right to teach and to speak publicly. Fell had Elizabeth I, the French regent Catherine de' Medici, and Mary Queen of Scots to lend her role models, as well as a clearly articulated religious perspective as a Quaker that supported

14. Eisenmann, *Historical Dictionary*, 202.

15. Ibid., 202.

16. Bizzell and Herzberg, "Christine de Pizan," 542.

17. de Pizan, Christine, "From *The Book of the City of Ladies*," 545.

18. Ibid., 545.

the view of women as spiritual equals.[19] Bizzell and Herzberg write that in the seventeenth century the Quakers were the "most anti-hierarchical and individualistic of Protestant denominations," advocating and practicing sexual equality more than any other.[20] In Fell's time, with a social action agenda meant to argue on behalf of the "poor, prostitutes, slaves, and other abused groups . . . preaching sometimes shaded over into political oratory." English women such as Fell thought that God was deeply concerned with humanity and offended by social wrongs. They left American women an important legacy to embrace in their push for social reforms in the nineteenth century.

In Fell's most famous text, published in 1666 and published again with a postscript in 1667, called "Women's Speaking Justified, Proved, and Allowed by the Scriptures," she argued that Paul has provided several conflicting scriptures about women speaking and not speaking. In 1 Corinthians 11:3 and 4 he gives instructions for women to cover their heads while prophesying, but in 1 Corinthians 14 he says it is shameful for women to speak in church.[21] Like many others who would argue for equality after she did, she listed women of the Old and New Testaments who were leaders, prophetesses, and Christians. For example, she named Anna as the prophetess who saw Christ in the temple and who gave thanks to God, speaking publicly.[22] Fell wrapped up her lengthy argument with a postscript that revealed her frustration with her opponents: "And you dark priests, that are so mad against Womens [sic] Speaking and it's so grievous [sic] to you." She then offered her final list of biblical examples and ended with a reminder that it was Mary who taught Joseph about God's plan enacted through her and her body.[23] Thus, she recognized her enemies—especially those who claimed to be Christians as well—but still found the door to freedom in the God she loved.

Mary Astell (1666–1731), also British, famously argued for women's education in *A Serious Proposal to the Ladies*, published in 1694. Although Sutherland points out that her idea was not new, Astell shows her rhetorical skill in a quote that challenges Christianity's imposed limitations on women while affirming the desire to continue the practice of faith: "God

---

19. Bizzell and Herzberg, "Margaret Fell," 748–49.

20. Ibid., 749.

21. Fell, "Women's Speaking," 755.

22. Ibid., 757.

23. Ibid., 760.

does nothing in vain, he gives no power or Faculty which he has not allotted to some proportionate use, if therefore he has given to Mankind a Rational Mind, every individual Understanding ought to be employ'd in somewhat worthy of it."[24] From this perspective and an embrace of Descartes, Astell argued that women would be better mothers if they were educated and could work as teachers if they did not become mothers.[25] However, because there was a societal connection between women's public speaking and moral purity in her time—with women who spoke publicly being denounced as promiscuous and manly—Astell did not argue women should speak publicly, but said "The way to be good Orators is to be good Christians," leaving the advice open for women writers or male speakers to use as might be appropriate.[26]

Published in 1787 in Britain, Mary Wollstonecraft's pamphlet, *Thoughts on the Education of Daughters, with Reflections on Female Conduct in the More Important Duties of Life*, argued for a mother's role to be enhanced through education. Her ideas would be more fully sketched out in *A Vindication of the Rights of Woman*, published in 1792.[27] Today she is known as the first feminist and is widely read in women's studies. In her time, however, not many people respected her ideas, yet there were "notable exceptions," according to the *Stanford Encyclopedia of Philosophy*'s biography of her life and contributions. In any case, in chapter 12 on "National Education" in *A Vindication of the Rights of Woman*, she first argued that boys and young men should not be taught solely at home or sent away to boarding schools, but be taught, "on terms of equality," at day schools so they could avoid becoming "vain and effeminate."[28] However, the dangers of educating boys in day schools included the propagation of bad manners (sexism) that was encouraged "when a number of them pig together in the same bedchamber," and could only be remedied by allowing girls to learn beside them so that everyone would use his and her best manners and learn how to treat each other properly. Later, like Wollstonecraft, American women would echo complaints about young women who loved pleasure, excess, and a "childish attachment to toys," and suggest that education for

24. Sutherland, "Mary Astell," 102.

25. Ibid., 100.

26. Ibid., 102, 112.

27. Tomaselli, "Mary Wollstonecraft."

28. Wollstonecraft, *Vindication of the Rights*, ch. 12.

both male and female, rich and poor, was the only real cure. Wollstonecraft went on to say:

> I know that libertines will also exclaim, that woman would be un-sexed by acquiring strength of body and mind, and that beauty, soft bewitching beauty! would no longer adorn the daughters of men. I am of a very different opinion, for I think that, on the contrary, we should then see dignified beauty and true grace; to produce which, many powerful physical and moral causes would concur. Not relaxed beauty, it is true, or the graces of helplessness; but such as appears to make us respect the human body as a majestic pile fit to receive a noble inhabitant, in the relics of antiquity.[29]

Like Emma Willard would later argue in her 1819 plan for the education of women, Wollstonecraft felt that these schools should be funded by the government, allowing equal opportunity for all. Finally, while many argued for the improvement of women only, Wollstonecraft, in her scathing, dramatic style points out the obvious—the problems with one half of the human race could only be addressed when the other half was improved as well: "Make them [women] free, and they will quickly become wise and virtuous, as men become more so, for the improvement must be mutual, or the injustice which one-half of the human race are obliged to submit to retorting on their oppressors, the virtue of man will be worm-eaten by the insect whom he keeps under his feet."[30]

Finally, one last British proponent of education is worth nothing. In 1799, Hannah More published *Strictures on the Modern System of Female Education*.[31] Vigorously criticizing the women of her time who were more interested in fashion and consumption than in virtue and in being proper mothers, More wrote: "But the great object to which you, who are, or may be mothers, are more especially called, is the education of your children," thereby presenting her best arguments for the education of women in terms of their need for moral improvement and in the idealized role of motherhood.[32] These are arguments that are reinvented in the social discourse about education for women over the next few decades.

29. Ibid.
30. Ibid.
31. More, "Chapter 1," 288.
32. Ibid., 306.

American Roots: Education for Men

Themes from the same arguments that led to opening colleges for men would be used to help women gain access to education that stretched beyond basic literacy and ornamental arts. Thus, the arguments for educating American men are an important antecedent to the arguments for educating American women in the eighteenth and nineteenth centuries. Historians Volo and Volo note that the colonies very much wanted to open colleges for young men, having grown tired of the expense of sending their children to school in England for "a decade or more" of their young lives.[33] The first eleven universities were: Harvard (1636), Yale (1701), Princeton (the College of New Jersey, 1746), the University of Pennsylvania (the Charity School of Philadelphia opened in 1751 as a branch of the Academy, College, and Charitable School of Philadelphia opened by Ben Franklin),[34] Columbia (King's College, 1754). Brown (1764), Rutgers (1766), Dartmouth (1770), William and Mary (1693), Transylvania College (1780), and Hampden-Sydney (1775).[35] "The immediate goal of the founders of Harvard was to produce a new generation of preachers, 'dreading to leave an illiterate ministry to the churches when our present ministers shall lie in the dust.'"[36] The other universities were opened for similar reasons, but Hampden-Sydney also cites its political fervor, which is not surprising considering the year it opened. Their passion for both God and country is evident in the first two paragraphs on their "About H-SC" webpage:

> Hampden-Sydney began as the southernmost representative of the "Log College" form of higher education established by the Scotch-Irish Presbyterians in America, whose academic ideal was the University of Edinburgh, seat of the Scottish Enlightenment. The first president, at the suggestion of Dr. John Witherspoon, the Scottish president of the College of New Jersey (now Princeton University), chose the name Hampden-Sydney to symbolize devotion to the principles of representative government and full civil and religious freedom which John Hampden (1594–1643) and Algernon Sydney (1622–1683) had outspokenly supported, and for which they had given their lives, in England's two great constitutional crises of the previous century. They were widely invoked

33. Volo and Volo, *Family Life*, 100.
34. University Archives and Records Center, "The Charity School."
35. Volo and Volo, 101; Hampden-Sydney College, "About H-SC."
36. Volo and Volo, 101.

as hero-martyrs by American colonial patriots, and their names immediately associated the College with the cause of independence championed by James Madison, Patrick Henry, and other less well-known but equally vigorous patriots who composed the College's first Board of Trustees. Indeed, the original students eagerly committed themselves to the revolutionary effort, organized a militia-company, drilled regularly, and went off to the defenses of Williamsburg, and of Petersburg, in 1777 and 1778 respectively. Their uniform of hunting-shirts—dyed purple with the juice of pokeberries—and grey trousers justifies the College's traditional colors, garnet and grey.[37]

These same patriotic ideals, reflected in the new concept of Republican Motherhood, strongly propelled society towards acceptance of a woman's need for higher education. According to the National Women's History Museum, not only did society see the education of women as ensuring the success of the new country, but it allowed women to engage in some civic activities.[38]

The political purposes for educating men can also be seen in the arguments made by our first president. In "The Cornerstone of the Republic: George Washington and the National University," Ryan Staude argues that it was Washington's own "modest" education and the arguments arising from the *American Museum* magazine, with notably influential people such as Benjamin Rush, that led Washington to desire a national university for men instead of continuing the practice of men going abroad for an education.[39] He was particularly concerned with educating men in military science and in "political training."[40] Citing the most common theme about education at all levels in the United States in the aftermath of the Revolutionary War, Staude writes that "a proper educational system was the best method of instilling the correct values and knowledge within Americans so they would be receptive to republicanism."[41] Again, Americans sought to educate the people because it was in the people's hands that the success of their new government rested.

While Washington and other proponents of the national university were never successful (colonies, and later states, opened their own

37. Hampden-Sydney College, "About H-SC."
38. National Women's History Museum, "Women's Changing Roles."
39. Staude, "The Cornerstone of the Republic," 38–39.
40. Ibid., 39–40.
41. Ibid., 35.

universities), it is important to see that the idea for women's education, justified by their political roles as mothers who would inculcate republican values in their sons and daughters, came from these arguments. An excerpt from Washington's eighth annual message to Congress given on December 7, 1796, is particularly illustrative:

> True it is that our country, much to its honor, contains many seminaries of learning highly respectable and useful; but the funds upon which they rest are too narrow to command the ablest professors in the different departments of liberal knowledge for the institution contemplated, thought they would be excellent auxiliaries. Amongst the motives to such an institution [the national university], the assimilation of the principles, opinions and manners of our countrymen by the common education of a portion of our youth from every quarter well deserves attention. The more homogeneous our citizens can be made in these particulars the greater will be our prospect of permanent union; and a primary object of such a National Institution should be the education of our youth in the science of *government*. In a Republic what species of knowledge can be equally important and what duty more pressing on its legislature than to patronize a plan for communicating it to those who are to be the future guardians of the liberty of the Country?[42]

It was only a short inductive leap to see women as the country's "future guardians" since they protected the countries youngest future republicans. Furthermore, just as with so much of our American government, this view must have been drawn from Greek and Roman intellectual fathers such as Aristotle who argued in *Politics* that the family is the model of the state; in fact, it is the state that draws together a structure for these families to exist and to move toward a common political enterprise. These ideas provided important roots for the education and, later, the empowerment, of women.

Shifting Epistemologies

Another important antecedent of female education can be found in the ideological shifts that shaped society. Mark Noll writes in *America's God* that the period of 1760–1820 was a time of "dramatic changes."[43] These changes were shifting dimensions of the ideological structure of the times, and these

42. Ibid., 50–1.
43. Noll, *America's God*, 214.

shifts led to arguments that women should be educated.[44] Broadly speaking, the factors in this new epistemology had its roots in changing ideas about "virtue" and this "not only helped reconcile classical republicanism with modernity and commerce; it laid the basis for all reform movements of the nineteenth century."[45] The factors of this new definition included:

1. "Democratization," or a change from the idea that actions benefitting the public could only come from the elite to the idea that these actions could be taken by "free white men;"

2. "A liberal concept of government," or an embrace of the idea that a "benevolent government" is a result of interested, active citizens who keep the powers of others "in check;"

3. "The new moral philosophy," or a change in the perspective that moral behavior was a result of reason to one that it was a result of emotion;

4. "The spread of sentimental literature," or the idea that women's chastity must be protected "against the conniving conspiracies of aggressive males;"

5. "Evangelicalization," or the idea that conversion was "a new sense of the heart," not the head;

6. And "the growth of a republican market mentality," or the idea that the "maintenance of personal virtue cultivated by wives and mothers in homes, schools, and churches" would not allow the moral issues associated with "personal gain" to get out of control."[46]

Noll quotes Ruth Bloch to show the connection between politics, social roles, and women's education: "What did change as a specific consequence of the American Revolutionary experiences was that the feminine notion of virtue took on a political significance it had previously lacked."[47] Mary Beth Norton, a historian, explains, "prior to the revolution, Americans paid little attention to the formal education of women," but "in the new republic, by contrast, the importance of female education was repeatedly emphasized."[48] She goes on to say,

44. Ibid., 214; Norton, *Liberty's Daughters*, 256.
45. Noll, *America's God*, 215.
46. Ibid., 215.
47. Ibid.
48. Norton, *Liberty's Daughters*, 256.

The Americans' vision of the ideal woman—an independent thinker and patriot, a wife, competent household manager, and knowledgeable mother—required formal instruction in a way that the earlier paragon, the notable housewife, did not. Moreover, Americans' wartime experiences convinced them that women needed broader training to prepare them for unseen contingencies.

Along with patriotism, we see over and over again the role war played in the rise of social justice for women. During times of war, women took over the duties of men successfully and competently. Most commonly noted in women's histories is how women stepped into jobs vacated by men during World War II, but these actions are similar to what women did as far back as the Revolutionary War.

Conclusion: "The Glory of Each Generation is to Make Its Own Precedents"[49]

To conclude, it is interesting to look back to our earliest American history to see how women acted in roles outside of their "sphere" from the very beginning in what would become the United States. In 1607 Jamestown was settled by men and by 1608 women began to join them there. One way that women were allowed to act outside their sphere was in a substitute leadership role. In this raw, unsettled country, women were able to run the farms, tend cattle, or do whatever else was necessary when their husbands were gone.[50] Interestingly, women who could hold off on marriage could retain their legal rights. Thus we have the story of Margaret and Mary Brent who chose to retain their freedom by refusing marriage in a "land of woman-starved bachelors."[51] America was a new place and could be described as sparsely populated if only white settlers were to be counted. There were only about four hundred settlers at that time. Taking with them a letter granting them land in their own names, the Brent sisters took hold of a seventy-one acre plot, later named "Sisters' Freehold." It was located in what is now southern Maryland. As a successful landowner, Margaret took the role of businesswoman, making loans to new settlers and rushing to take anyone to court who failed to pay his debt. Later, she became America's first lawyer

49. "Belva Ann Lockwood," http://www.biography.com/people/belva-lockwood-9384624#awesm=~oI3RLNQ2ULhzev.

50. Brekus, *Strangers and Pilgrims*, 12.

51. Ibid.

when Governor Calvert appointed her executor of his estate, and she became the first woman to demand the right to vote on January 21, 1648 when she went before the Maryland Assembly as a landowner in her own right and as a landowner in Calvert's stead.[52] If she were a man, she would have had all she needed to be granted the right to vote. Despite the challenges, her life is another example of how women in the New World were sometimes able to capitalize on their circumstances to live as equals to men.

Of course, the economic rights enjoyed by women like the Brents were only temporary. Most women would find it necessary to work within the "sphere" of home long after their time. There, they did not contribute by choice but by necessity. However, by making the very most of this role, they would one day gain their freedom from its restrictions.

The Brents demonstrate an American spirit that runs through our history. Centuries later, another woman would use her role as a lawyer to be the first to run for president in 1884, attempting to enjoy her full rights just as the Brents tried to do.[53] By ignoring societal restrictions just as the Brent sisters once did, Belva Lockwood obtained her law degree first by studying privately while applying to various colleges. She finally was accepted to National University Law School in 1871 when it began to allow women to enroll. Like Margaret Brent, Lockwood did not accept the law that denied women the right to appear before the Supreme Court and had a new law passed to allow her to appear in court in 1889. Lockwood worked to secure equal property and voting rights for women in the 1880s and 90s. Born in New York in 1830, she passed away in Washington, DC in 1917.[54] The link between Lockwood and the Brent sisters lies in access to education, not just to changing ideas about women's roles. Her education and experience allowed her to run for our country's highest office.

Today, access to higher education has allowed women the option of working in the home, outside of the home, or a blend of the two. When we say "work outside of the home," it connotes so much more than just the ability to earn money in the public sphere. As our American ancestors such

52. Ibid., 14.

53. Jerry L. Clark, archivist, mentioned this during a presentation at the Cherokee Heritage Conference, June 2014. Lockwood is also known for going before the Supreme Court in 1906 and obtaining a five million dollar settlement for the Cherokee people. One quote attributed to her is: "I know we can't abolish prejudice through laws, but we can set up guidelines by legislation."

54. "Belva Ann Lockwood," http://www.biography.com/people/belva-lockwood-9384624#awesm=~oI3RLNQ2ULhzev.

as the Brent sisters and Belva Lockwood demonstrate, working outside of the home meant that women had an opportunity to change the world for the better. Today, women take for granted their freedom to vote, to own property, to use high-quality childcare, to count on high-quality senior care for aging parents, to divorce, to have legal recourse against physical and sexual abuse (even if it's from their husbands), to be treated with respect in the workplace, to engage in political activities, to preach, to hold high positions within the church and in businesses, to own their own businesses and to expect to keep their own wages, and so on. These freedoms have become a part of American culture and because they are a part of our way of life, they have become protected to a large degree. Our greatest debt is to those who supplied the key that led to these freedoms, that is, to those who fought for women to obtain an education equal to that afforded to men.

2

Political and Religious Roots: The "Fourth Branch of Government" and Early Exhorters

The "Fourth Branch of Government"

EDUCATION FOR WOMEN WAS deeply rooted in the ideals of womanhood, often summed up in three categories by historians that represent the chronological progression in the views of womanhood in the United States: The Colonial Good Wife, the Republican Mother, and the True Woman. The transition from colonial "Good Wife" to "Republican Motherhood" and later to the nineteenth-century "True Woman" was characterized by descriptions of how woman's moral character and influence were perceived.[1] "For the Puritan Good Wife," a woman was to exhibit wisdom in a religious sense, but for the "Republican Mother," a woman was to exhibit wisdom in a political sense.[2] Historian Susan Lindley quotes Linda Kerber as saying, "Motherhood was discussed almost as if it were a fourth branch of government, a device that ensured social control in the gentlest possible way."[3] Yet, it would be a mistake to separate the religious disposition of the Good Wife from that of the Republican Mother. While varying amounts of attention were given to a woman's function, Lindley writes that "we must be careful not to separate too sharply 'political' and 'religious' spheres or functions."[4]

1. Lindley, *You have Stept*, 50–52.
2. Ibid., 51.
3. Ibid., 52.
4. Ibid., 51.

Also, although religion was an obvious type of social control, a sincerely felt relationship with God was often the pathway to spiritual peace and freedom within any social or political context. In fact, a crucial component for women's social emancipation came from women working to subvert the religious structures that tried to prohibit equality—not by turning away from God—but by providing an exegetical perspective that allowed for new hermeneutics to reveal that the Bible was not meant to limit but to liberate.

Indeed, the eighteenth-century birth of educational reform was part of a three-pronged argument that rested comfortably within Christianity. First, proponents argued that education would not "unsex" women but make them better wives and mothers; second, they emphasized the effects of education on good behavior; and third, they emphasized that the "requirements of republican citizenship" justified changing the educational goals for women.[5] A 1787 address given to the Philadelphia Young Ladies' Society by Benjamin Rush revealed another key aspect of this new desire to educate women, "[F]emale education," he said, "should be accommodated to the state of society, manners, and government" of the United States, and it should be "conducted upon principles very different from what it was in Great Britain, and in some respects different from what it was when we were part of a monarchical empire."[6] Thus, educating women was a symbol of the break from Great Britain; it was evidence of the new way of life Americans were in the process of defining. It would be, of course, better than what they or the generation before had left behind—a major component of the new American ethnocentric ideology that still characterizes us today.

Admittedly, in colonial America and later in the New Republic, the realities of women's lives did not leave much room for the pursuit of an education in the lower classes. For example, colonial housewives worked to create cloth which was in drastically short supply in the seventeenth century. When not spinning, they made soap, planted gardens, made cheese, made butter, and worked as midwives. Since most women were pregnant a good deal of the time and might have as many as seven children (the reported average), working as a wet nurse was another occupation for women, adding considerably to a constant state of exhaustion.[7] They bartered with each other and enjoyed a type of economic control because their work made

5. Norton, *Liberty's Daughters*, 265.
6. Ibid., 267–68.
7. Ibid., 55.

them necessary, but they were probably too tired to care about the merits of the kinds of economic power they were allowed to wield.[8]

By the eighteenth century, however, imported goods made life easier for women.[9] As women became less valuable as unpaid laborers, they quickly turned to emphasizing their role as mothers and teachers instead. These roles allowed them more room to control some aspects of their lives they had less time or energy for previously.[10] As they were needed less at home, many women desired an income. One acceptable role was as a teacher. Thus, their role as teachers in Dame schools, common schools, boarding houses, and in the female academies and seminaries that began to flourish in the late eighteenth and early nineteenth century were a big part of all that allowed them to eventually obtain equal rights to an education. Unlike the women of the upper classes, who justified their need for an education in terms of a desire for an "ornamental" education in needlework, painting, and later in terms of a desire to create good citizens out of their children and who had been enjoying something of an education since colonial times, the women of the lower classes would do so by working as teachers, catching up with their more affluent sisters in the nineteenth century as quickly as time and necessity would allow.

Religious Roots: Women Preachers

Besides teaching, another role that opened the door for women was that of preacher, exhorter, prophetess—call it what you will. The religious fervor associated with the Great Awakening between the 1730s and the 1770s allowed for both women and African Americans to participate in religious gatherings in new ways,[11] and the revivals of the Second Great Awakening in the early nineteenth century, which, according to Donald Scott of Queens College, "has to be understood as a vast and powerful religious movement,"[12] allowed for women to become preachers due to a shift away from the belief that an education was needed to properly prepare a preacher to the idea that only the right "heart" was needed. Women preachers increased in numbers in the nineteenth century, holding leadership roles dur-

8. Ibid., 51.
9. Ibid., 68.
10. Ibid., 69.
11. Heyrman, "The First Great Awakening."
12. Scott, "Evangelicalism."

ing the same time that other women were entering into teaching and school administration, into politics, and into the civic sphere as reformers who petitioned for change within prisons, orphanages, mental institutions, and so on. Scott points out that "By the 1820s evangelicalism had become one of the most dynamic and important cultural forces in American life." The rise of social justice for women is therefore intimately tied to the mutability of the American religious experience and the transformation of exegetical practices that accompanied it. More so than the secular roles that women held, assuming the role of spiritual leader—in whatever shape it took—was an incredibly important proponent of the empowerment of women, as evidence of their excellence, in a society that openly valued Christianity in most if not all major social institutions, including government.

Ironically, women entered into preaching not by justifying their right to an education so they would be qualified to enter it but by claiming that an education, which barred them from preaching, was not needed in order to become a preacher. Mark Noll, the Francis A. McAnaney Professor of History at the University of Notre Dame, notes that a distrust of "intellectual authorities" was shared by most eighteenth-century Americans.[13] The distrust of formal education handed to nineteenth-century Americans was due to a "belief that true knowledge arose from the use of one's own senses." He writes: "Most Americans were thus united in the conviction that they had to think for themselves in order to know science, morality, economics, politics, and especially theology." Rooted in the "common sense" theories of the Scottish Enlightenment, knowledge was a "product of epistemological self-assertion that heeded no creed but the Bible."[14] Notably, Methodists, who licensed women preachers in the nineteenth century, are named by Noll as an example of those embracing this epistemological perspective.[15] Also, during the Great Awakening of the 1740s, Gilbert Tennet criticized educated clergymen who weren't converted but felt qualified to preach by giving more weight to the religious experiences of preachers than to their education.[16] Although his attacks were aimed at men, his criticism had far-reaching benefits for women. Now able to claim spiritual authority was not dependent upon a traditional education, women began to claim and to exercise the most respected kind of authority—that is, religious au-

13. Noll, *America's God*, 11.

14. Ibid., 11–12.

15. Ibid., 12.

16. Brekus, *Strangers and Pilgrims*, 33, 37.

thority—and the new American Eden began to change once more. Even though women like Anne Hutchinson and Mary Dyer left chilling legacies of defeat, new progress was made for women's social equality in the fires of these revivals that allowed for women to spontaneously enter into spiritual leadership roles.

The idea that a formal education was not needed in order to know God or to speak for God is biblical, but not because Christians did not value intellectual development, but because they had access to a greater source of knowledge. Grounded in a Pauline ethos, for the preacher/orator knowledge was built through intimacy with God and humility, not through education, expertise, or rhetorical technique in speaking. The knowledge that was valued was that of God's wisdom, and the preacher's job was to communicate that knowledge to others. The preacher was to share "God's hidden wisdom" as it was "revealed" through the Spirit because the "spirit explores everything, even the depths of God's own nature" (1 Cor 2:7–10).[17] Therefore, the preacher interpreted "spiritual truths to those who have the Spirit" and spoke "of these gifts of God in words taught us not by our human wisdom but by the Spirit" (1 Cor 2:13). The "debater," as a representative of those rhetoricians with secular educations, was described as one who is full of worldly knowledge and expertise (1 Cor 1:20). By using these scriptures to shift away from education as the qualification for ministry, women could enter into leadership positions previously closed to them.

Long before the Methodists, Quaker women in colonial America acted out the social rights given to them through their religion. However, this is not to say that women became preachers without any opposition. Puritans supported sexist social paradigms—although Brekus notes that they did argue for a woman's spiritual equality.[18] When the idea of a spiritual mother was confined to the home, the Puritans were comfortable with the idea and supported spiritual equality. But when the idea of a spiritual mother was enacted as a prophetess, woman preacher, or even as someone allowed to simply speak as an authority within the church, it was a threat.

For example, we have the story of the Quaker Anne Hutchinson (1591–1643) who began holding women's club meetings at her house despite societal pressures. According to the *Encyclopaedia Britannica*,

> She married William Hutchinson, a merchant, in 1612, and in 1634 they migrated to Massachusetts Bay Colony. Anne Hutchinson

17. *The Oxford English Study Bible.*
18. Brekus, *Strangers and Pilgrims*, 31.

soon organized weekly meetings of Boston women to discuss recent sermons and to give expression to her own theological views. Before long her sessions attracted ministers and magistrates as well. She stressed the individual's intuition as a means of reaching God and salvation, rather than the observance of institutionalized beliefs and the precepts of ministers. Her opponents accused her of antinomianism—the view that God's grace has freed the Christian from the need to observe established moral precepts.[19]

Brekus notes that her meetings were well attended, but she did not go unpunished for defying social conventions and the dominant religion of her day.[20] Brought up on charges, at her trial she claimed to have merely repeated the content of Sunday sermons. John Winthrop's diary records the accusation clearly: "Shee [sic] would comment upon the Doctrines and expound dark places of scripture."[21] After trying her before the town government, imprisoning her in the home of Joseph Weld for a year (1637–8), and trying her before the Boston Church,[22] they chose to exile this "American Jezebel" to Rhode Island.[23]

Another example of a woman who defied societal restrictions but did not reject Christianity is Mary Dyer. She turned from Puritanism to Quakerism and began to speak publicly, "witnessing" to others.[24] The Puritans put her on trial and tried to keep her in exile, but finally hanged her in 1660 when she refused both silence and submission.

Women did not always experience such dire consequences for preaching. An interesting example of an early woman preacher is Bathsheba Kingsley of Westfield, Massachusetts who spent two years evangelizing people

19. "Anne Hutchinson." In *Encyclopaedia Brittanica*: http://www.britannica.com/EBchecked/topic/277653/Anne-Hutchinson.

20. Brekus, *Strangers and Pilgrims*, 31.

21. Ibid., 31.

22. "Anne Hutchinson." In *Encyclopaedia Brittanica*: http://www.britannica.com/EBchecked/topic/277653/Anne-Hutchinson.

23. Brekus, *Strangers and Pilgrims*, 31, 32. For those unaware of the significance of this label, Jezebel was the one who controlled King Ahab, King of Israel, and turned the Israelites away from worshipping God. She murdered all of God's priests that she could find. It wasn't until the prophet Elijah confronted her in a famous stand off between him and God the 450 prophets of Baal, as described in 1 Kgs 18, that the tide began to turn and Israel was able to come back to God. Her death is described in 2 Kgs 9. She is trampled by horses and eaten by dogs so that there was only her skull, hands, and feet left that could be buried. She was a sworn, active enemy of God.

24. Ibid., 30.

by going from "house to house."[25] The famous preacher Jonathan Edwards was part of an ecclesiastical council called to deal with the problem of Kingsley, called together in 1743 to address the situation. A modern day sort of Socrates, she was accused of singling out people she felt were in need of moral correction, including ministers. Her accusations posed a very real threat to the hierarchical social order in place by undermining the authority of the men who were probably accustomed to not being questioned. The council advised her to continue her ministry but to not claim the authority of a minister. In an effort to control her, they told her to stay home instead of traveling about.[26] Although she was ultimately controlled, her actions challenged boundaries.

A few decades after that and coinciding with the Revolutionary Period, we have the example of another woman who actually managed to circumvent misogyny to some degree. Sarah Wright Townsend preached almost every Sunday in a Long Island Separate church without challenge for about fifteen years before her own son-in-law tried to convince the church to affiliate with the "Regular" Baptists. His attempts failed and her church did not unite with them until 1789. This was about nine years after her death.[27]

The most interesting figure of Revolutionary America was Jemima Wilkinson, aka the Publick Universal Friend, known as P.U.F. for short.[28] Unlike more tame examples of women who merely wished to preach or teach, Jemima claimed to have literally died and risen again as someone who was literally neither male nor female. Allowed to dress as a man, she was invited to preach in several mainstream churches during the height of her popularity.[29] Even so, by the 1790s, her ministry had withered away despite her enormous popularity. She died in 1819, buried in a tomb with the name Publick Universal Friend engraved on the front.[30]

Ann Lee, a contemporary of P.U.F., began her career around 1776, the same time Jemima did. Like P.U.F., she founded her own religious sect in western New York.[31] However, unlike P.U.F., she was illiterate. She required her followers to be celibate in order to be considered as "saved," and she led

---

25. Ibid., 24.
26. Ibid., 25, 26.
27. Ibid., 59, 60.
28. Ibid., 86.
29. Ibid., 91.
30. Ibid., 96- 97.
31. Ibid., 97.

her followers in ecstatic "singing, dancing, trembling, and whirling" instead of offering them formal guidance through sermons. Brekus writes "Before Lee died in 1784 . . . they [she and her followers] danced 'stark naked together' (to symbolize their religious purity), burned books and furniture, performed faith healings, drank to excess, and exorcised demons."[32] In opposition to these women and to the revivals of the first Great Awakening in general, the "Old Lights" said that any "misguided," demon-possessed woman who wanted to speak in public simply wanted to "'usurp' their husband's authority so they could be 'Queens for Life.'"[33]

Although these particular examples do not represent the norm for women in society, they had much more "normal" contemporaries. In the nineteenth century, the Methodists would be famous for their female itinerant preachers, the most famous of whom is the evangelist Phoebe Palmer, and her well-known contemporaries who freely married religion and social reform: the Methodist Frances Willard, President of the WCTU (Woman's Christian Temperance Union) and the Methodist Catherine Booth, co-founder of the Salvation Army. Later, Pentecostals of the early twentieth century are noted for the profusion of women preachers who were transformed by the Azusa Street revivals. For three years, from 1906–1908, these were led by an African American man, William Seymour, son of former slaves. He was assisted by former slave, woman preacher, and descendent of the great Frederick Douglass, Lucy Farrow.[34] Thus, Pentecostalism in the twentieth century was birthed out of gender and racial equality, a fact well documented by scholars such as Dr. Vinson Synan.[35] Out of Pentecostalism, we have other twentieth-century celebrities such as Aimee Semple McPherson who was herself radical, changing the nature of American religion by her flamboyant preaching and dramatic, larger-than-life style.

Ironic Progress

To sum up, the role of women preachers in the fight to obtain an education for women is an ironic one. The insistence on using common sense over education was a major factor in obtaining the right to an equal education for women. The insistence by some, who like Gilbert who criticized the

32. Ibid., 103.
33. Ibid., 39.
34. Cauchi, "Lucy F. Farrow."
35. Synan, *The Century of the Holy Spirit.*

male preachers of his time who believed that education need not be the only qualification for ministry, pushed women forward. Since Christianity was the lifeblood of America for the first two centuries or so, women stepping into roles as preachers and prophetesses set an example of God-given power, and their influence cannot be overstated. In Welch's exploration of ethos and selected late nineteenth, twentieth, and twenty-first–century Pentecostal women preachers, she discovered that the combination of a call story, the baptism in the Holy Spirit, and the anointing to preach were based in a Pauline epistemology that gave them more legitimacy and staying power than Gilbert's criticisms.[36] Using their ethos, Pentecostal women preachers established credibility through the combination of these three experiences and the scriptures that supported them. They used their ethos to establish themselves as a voice of wisdom and authority in the church, allowing the Holy Spirit to speak through them and to transform their congregations. As a tool of transformation, the power obtained through radical submission to Christ was ironic for how it was obtained, but instructive in how it shifted the dynamics away from a human patriarchy to a spiritual hierarchy that allowed women to be respected in one of the highest callings we can obtain in this life. Women entering into the pulpit pushed forward the rise of social equality all women, beginning as far back as the seventeenth century in America and stretching into the present day. The connections between women preachers and the rise of social equality for women begs for more exploration.

Additionally, it is also an often-noted irony that women gained the right to an equal education partially because of an insistence that women fill idealized roles within the home, allowing them to attend schools for more than just basic literacy. This theme fills the research of scholars who research the history of women and higher education in the United States. Leonard Sweet writes that between 1820 and 1850 Americans had shifted to support the education of women. This had culminated in the belief that "women were viewed as under a special obligation to develop their mental powers to the fullest."[37] As the ideal for womanhood moved from the Republican Mother toward the "True Woman," this was to support them in their roles as mothers and as wives, but it advanced their position nonetheless. This paradox is noted in Lindley and in Norton. Lindley writes that "pioneer educators" like Emma Willard, the founder of the Troy

---

36. Welch, *Women with the Good News*.

37. Sweet, "Female Seminary," 41.

Female Seminary, Mary Lyon, the founder of Mount Holyoke Seminary, and Catharine Beecher, founder of Hartford Seminary, supported the idea that education helped women better perform their assigned duties and that their "efforts were unintentionally subversive to tradition."[38] It is why, as Lindley notes and as Susie Stanley echoes in *Holy Boldness*, some have dismissed them as "antifeminist."[39] Even so, as Norton writes, "Paradoxically . . . the first major breach in the conventional feminine role was justified by reference to that role itself."[40] Also, it is ironic that women gained the right to an equal education partially because of an insistence that colleges train men for political reasons, not just to prepare them for the ministry. Because of this shift in emphasis for men's education, the birth of Republican Motherhood began to open doors for women in the realms of higher education.

Finally, it is ironic in light of contemporary scholarship that liberal feminists owe such a great debt to Christians. The rise of social justice for women is sometimes framed in the history of women who rejected Christianity, but many Christian women of the eighteenth and nineteenth centuries found a way to make equality compatible with religion, much as they do today. These women were far more influential than those who rejected Christianity and their influence was not recognized until the last few decades as feminist scholars have revised history to fit their desired social, political, and anti-religious paradigms. Yet while Christian feminists have often been less vocal than their liberal counterparts in recent decades, which is partially due to the well-documented expulsion of conservatives from some disciplines in the universities (search "conservatives and liberals" in *The Chronicle of Higher Education*), their influence is still vital for the propagation of social values that embrace equality in our time.

In fact, scholars such as Ruelas have begun the work to recover histories other feminists have ignored. In his book *Women and the Landscape of Higher Education: Wesleyan Holiness and Pentecostal Founders*, he recaptures the stories of no less than thirty-one Christian women who started either Bible schools or colleges between 1855 and 1970, with the majority of these falling between 1900 and 1930.[41] Historians have largely forgotten famous names such as Carrie Judd Montgomery, who began the Shalom Training School in 1894, Mattie Mallory who began Beulah Heights Col-

---

38. Lindley, *You Have Stept*, 91.

39. Ibid., 91; Stanley, *Holy Boldness*, 10.

40. Norton, *Liberty's Daughters*, 193.

41. Ruelas, *Women and the Landscape*, 151–53.

lege and Bible School in 1906 (now Southern Nazarene University), Alma White who began Zarephath Bible Institute in 1908 (now Somerset Christian College), Nora Chambers who began a Bible Training School in 1918 (now Lee University), Aimee Semple McPherson who began Echo Park Evangelistic and Missionary Training Institute in 1923 (now Life Pacific College), and Bebe Patten who began Oakland Bible Institute in 1944 (now Patten University). As we piece together the history of women's rise to social equality, it is important not to ignore the continuing influence of Christian women who hold a variety of leadership positions, not only in the church but in society at large.

3

Religious and Cultural Sources for the Founding of Female Seminaries: From "Butterflies to Eagles"

Private Tutors, Common Schools, and Boarding Houses: Education and the First Ladies of the White House

HOW WERE WOMEN EDUCATED in the Revolutionary Period? In the eighteenth century, many boys and girls were educated separately and many had private tutors in the home. The education of the First Ladies of the White House demonstrates the types of education both available and acceptable from the Revolutionary Period forward. It illustrates the variety of educational opportunities available and the actual accomplishments of the women who took advantage of those opportunities. Demonstrating a wide variety, their education shows a non-systematic approach to education that characterized the early United States. Although, as Stephen Robertson writes, "women were expected to conform to an ideal of passive purity that did not include participation in the sordid world of politics," these women set the pace for their peers and became idealized examples for the lower classes.[1] Regardless of their political involvement or restraint, if women in the White House were educated, then women in American homes would also wish to be educated, emulating the highest rungs of the social ladder as fully as possible.

1. Robertson, "Biographies of the First Ladies," 145.

The kinds of education the First Ladies received varied, but show the progression of women's education from private tutor to college over the eighteenth and nineteenth centuries. For example, several First Ladies of the White House who were born in the eighteenth century were tutored privately. While Letitia Tyler's education is unknown, Martha Washington, Abigail Adams, Martha Jefferson, Dolley Madison, Elizabeth Monroe, Rachel Jackson, and Margaret Taylor learned at home. These home educations varied in quality.[2] Martha Washington was terrible at spelling and is remembered as not being very well read, so her education must have been lacking.[3] Abigail Adams used her family's library to educate herself but later learned Latin and taught her children Latin soon after.[4] As an exception to the "non-participation" rule concerning women and politics, Adams attempted to bring about change for women at the highest level of government. In a now famous letter to her husband, John, on August 14, 1776, she argued that women should be educated:

> If you complain of neglect of education in sons, what shall I say with regard to daughters, who every day experience the want of it? With regard to the education of my own children, I find myself soon out of my depth, and destitute and deficient in every part of education. . . . I most sincerely wish that some more liberal plan might be laid and executed for the benefit of the rising generation, and that our new constitution may be distinguished for learning and virtue. If we mean to have heroes, statesmen and philosophers, we should have learned women. The world perhaps would laugh at me, and accuse me of vanity, but you I know have a mind too enlarged and liberal to disregard the sentiment. If much depends as is allowed upon the early education of youth and the first principals which are instilled take the deepest root, great benefit must arise from literary accomplishments in women.[5]

Of course, most women who eventually occupied the White House had some form of education but perhaps not the kind Adams longed for. Instead, they learned to read and write and to run a household, often overseeing slaves, but they also learned sewing, music, painting, needlework, and home

---

2. National First Ladies' Library, "First Ladies Research."
3. Robertson, "Biographies of the First Ladies," 150.
4. Ibid., 151.
5. Adams, "Letter from Abigail Adams."

remedies for illnesses.[6] In addition to these types of education, First Lady Rachel Jackson was especially known as an accomplished horsewoman.

Women of the White House who were born in either the eighteenth or the nineteenth century were often educated at home, sometimes in combination with a local school. For example, Hannah Hoes Van Buren was educated at a local school in Kinderhook, New York.[7] Likewise, Abigail Powers Fillmore was educated in a one-room schoolhouse in Sempronius, Cayuga County, New York from 1804 to 1814. Also educated at home, she became "proficient in math, government, history, philosophy and geography." Jane Means Appleton Pierce was taught at home but excelled at music. The details of Ellen Lewis Herndon Arthur's education are unknown; she could have either been taught at home or attended a local school in Washington, DC. Like many Americans of their time, while they were educated as children at local schools, these women did not have the benefit of education as they grew older.

As Americans became increasingly concerned with educating young women, boarding schools became popular. Boarding schools provided a more formal education, instructing the young women in arts, manners, and literature. The arts included "drawing, painting, music, and fancy needlework." The earliest First Lady known to have attended a boarding school was Louisa Catherine Johnson Adams.[8] The daughter-in-law of the famous Abigail Adams, she had to give up her two oldest sons to the care of Abigail (who did not really like her) for six years while her husband was sent to Russia as an ambassador between 1809 and 1815.[9] She was also the first President's wife born outside of the U.S. She first went to a Roman Catholic convent school in Nantes, France from 1781–1783. There, she "learned to read and write in French . . . to play the harp and piano, and to sing. After that, she spent five years in an English boarding school for girls from 1784–1789." She studied "mathematics, philosophy, embroidery, needlework, stitching, [and] drawing."[10] It is said that one teacher taught her to see outside of society's limitations, but since she had to live within those limitations, she questioned the wisdom of knowing the truth. Last, she had a private tutor in London from about 1789 to 1793. After that, she and her sisters left the boarding

6. National First Ladies' Library, "First Ladies Research."

7. Ibid.

8. National First Ladies' Library, "First Ladies Research."

9. Robertson, "Biographies of the First Ladies," 157.

10. National First Ladies' Library, "First Ladies Research."

school and Louisa took up writing poetry, essays, and playwriting.[11] While other first ladies exerted varying levels of political influence, she and her husband did not discuss politics.[12] She kept firmly out of the political arena by holding to her silence in this area. Other first ladies who attended boarding schools included Harriet Johnston and Julia Grant.[13]

Case in Point: Hannah Foster's The Boarding School

What did young women learn in the boarding schools? In 1798, Hannah Foster published *The Boarding School, or Lessons of a Preceptress to her Pupils*.[14] This book was designed to help the women who earned a living as one of these in-home teachers. Her book is written from the perspective of the fictitious teacher as a record of the lessons she gave in the final week of instruction at her home. In it, the chapters are divided into morning and evening lessons, and "Mrs. Williams" shaped her students' beliefs to match the prevailing ideologies of the time by telling frightening stories of girls who did horrible things, like become actresses, marry for love, or refuse to be practical minded about having a way to earn a living with a womanly activity like needlework, which might be needed in the event that a spouse should pass away.

In the book, Foster explains that Mrs. Williams, who was the "virtuous relict [widow] of a respectable clergyman" and a mother of two young daughters of her own, decided to open a boarding house—not for an income as her "circumstances were easy"—but "To cultivate the expanding flowers, and to prune the juvenile eccentricities, which were disseminated among these tender plants; or, to speak without a figure, to extend and purify their ideas, to elevate and refine their affections, to govern and direct their passions" for the seven young girls now in her care.[15] These girls were probably in their teenage years, and Mrs. Williams' duty was "to polish the mental part, to call forth the dormant virtues, to unite and arrange the charms of person and mind, to inspire a due sense of decorum and propriety, and to instil [sic] such principles of piety, morality, benevolence, prudence and economy, as might

---

11. Ibid.
12. Robertson, "Biographies of the First Ladies," 157.
13. National First Ladies' Library, "First Ladies Research."
14. Foster, *The Boarding School*.
15. Ibid., 5–6.

be useful through life."[16] In other words, she would make sure that the girls under her care properly reflected the social ideologies prevalent at the time. The girls would know their place in society and be well prepared to play their role in the home as a good wife and mother.

Rising at five, Foster explained that the girls breakfasted with Mrs. Williams at seven where she could observe "any indecorum of behavior, or wrong bias; which she kept in mind, until proper time to mention, and remonstrate against it; a method, the salutary effects of which were visible in the daily improvement of her students."[17] Their mornings were spent doing needlework, with one girl assigned to read to them for entertainment.[18] Each day, the one who had read them an "instructive" book would present her own composition in the afternoon, either in the form of prose or poetry. Mrs. Williams and the other girls would critique it in a discussion. Then, the girls could dance or sing or do whatever they wanted for the evening hours—so long as it was an activity appropriate for a girl to do.[19] In the very last week, however, Mrs. Williams wanted to spend her time summing up her "counsels, admonitions, and advice" in a series of monologues, replete with imaginative tales designed to entertain and to illustrate the veracity of her insights.[20] Each chapter records these lessons.

Her first lesson comes at the end of "The Boarding School, & c." In this lesson, a young girl who did not learn to sew ordinary items, just to do fancy needlework, was left without a way to generate income after her circumstances took a turn for the worse. In "Monday, P.M., Reading," the second lesson is about the dangers of reading novels and imagining that marriage is about romance instead of securing a good income.[21] Her example is a daughter who married for love, lost everything, and was the cause of her parent's heartbreak and subsequent poverty that resulted from their heartbreak. In contrast to the girls who failed, Mrs. Williams also tells the story of a girl who did learn needlework and manage to earn a living and

16. Ibid., 6.

17. Ibid., 8–9.

18. In a later chapter, I offer pieces of Emma Willard's "Plan" for educating young women, and she specifically points out that needlework consumes too much of a young woman's time and that there was little intellectual profit from it. Therefore, she eliminates it from the bulk of her suggested curriculum, allowing needlework and sewing little room.

19. Foster, *The Boarding School*, 9.

20. Ibid., 10.

21. Ibid., 15.

of a girl who read poetry and history and kept clear of novels and was very successful as a result.

In the section titled "Tuesday, A.M.," Mrs. Williams speaks about writing and math.[22] Writing is good, but can be dangerous if you put your true thoughts into a letter. In the story, the letters between two thought-less young girls voicing unacceptable ideas are made public by a man who would have been wonderful to marry. As a result, the girls are destroyed. She then told a story where a young woman had a wealthy father and so did not need to learn math to guide her finances. Of course, the father dies in this story and she ends up in poverty. The stories follow this pattern throughout the text. For example, in "Tuesday, P.M., Music and Dancing," it begins with instruction in how to participate in these activities properly:

> As dancing is an accomplishment merely external, let not the vanity of excellence in it betray itself in an air of conscious superiority, when you shine at the ball, and perceive yourselves to have attracted the attention and applause of the gay assembly. But in the midst of hilarity and mirth, remember that modesty, diffidence, discretion, and humility are indispensable appendages of virtue and decency.[23]

Mrs. Williams goes on to encourage the girls to dance and sing, even at the request of others. What is important is to keep the right attitude. To offer an example of how pride can take them astray, Mrs. Williams launches into the story of Levitia.

> Levitia was endowed, by the joint influence of nature and art, with these pleasing charms. Symmetry was perfected in her form; and her voice was melody itself. Her parents were not in affluent circumstances; yet their tastes led them to distinguish those graces and talents in their daughter, which they injudiciously flattered themselves might, one day, raise her to affluence and fame.[24]

In this example, Mrs. Williams clearly shows the importance of the kind of education she offers them. She expresses the belief that the poorer members of society might be able to instinctively exhibit good taste but would not know how to handle it if artistic gifts were evident in their daughters. Of course, the parents seek to pay for help in cultivating their

22. Ibid., 27.
23. Ibid., 36.
24. Ibid., 39.

daughter's talents and in the end "Flattery was appealing to her ear, in whatever form it was presented."[25] In other words, the girl did not have the good sense to know that flattery from "the licentious" was abhorrent. A foreigner now enters the story, offering her guidance and fame. Believing in his goodwill, she became "a professed actress."[26] "Her parents are overwhelmed with grief and anxiety, at the discovery; but to no purpose were all exertions to reclaim her." Instead, "She made her appearance on the stage. She sung and danced, for which she was caressed, flattered, paid." Here it is clear why Hannah Foster was so careful to be clear that Mrs. Williams did not open a boarding house for income, but out of the generosity of her soul. To be paid in the wrong way would be humiliating.

As for the daughter, "Her gaiety and beauty gained her many votaries, and she became a complete courtezan [sic]."[27] As a result, her mother "died of a broken heart," the daughter became ill and lost her beauty—the foreigner leaving her to "poverty and shame," and returning to her father, she finds him in poverty, unable to help either her or himself.[28] In contrast, Florella is "superior to the vain arts of flattery" and only engages in music and dancing to amuse her friends. "How happy her parents are in her filial duty and affection! How rich the reward of their care and expense in contributing to her improvements! How happy Florella in their complacency and love, and in the consciousness of deserving them!"[29] Indeed, how clearly the boarding school is needed for cultivating the right virtues in young women to save them from lives of trouble and destruction. Florella marries happily, of course.

Following this chapter is "Wednesday, A.M., Miscellaneous Directions, For the Government of the Temper and the Manners,"[30] "Wednesday, P.M., Dress,"[31] "Thursday, A.M., Politeness,"[32] "Thursday, P.M., Amusements,"[33]

25. Ibid., 40.
26. Ibid., 41.
27. Ibid.
28. Ibid., 41–42.
29. Ibid., 43.
30. Ibid., 44.
31. Ibid., 55.
32. Ibid., 60.
33. Ibid., 69.

"Friday, A.M., Filial and Fraternal Affection,"[34] "Friday, P.M., Friendship,"[35] "Saturday, A.M., Love,"[36] and "Saturday, P.M., Religion."[37] These follow a similar pattern to the one I have shared. Pages 103 to 228 are copies of letters from Mrs. Williams' students and her daughters Anna and Maria. Some are written to Mrs. Williams and some are correspondence between the young women. They demonstrate how the girls have applied all of her wisdom to their lives and testify to her effectiveness as a teacher. By demonstrating her competence in this way, Mrs. Williams is able to offer evidence that her boarding school is excellent without appearing arrogant. Of course, Mrs. Williams may never have actually existed, but would have served her purpose as a character designed to represent the work Hannah Foster did by running her own boarding school. By hiding behind Mrs. Williams, Hannah reserved her dignity and embraced humility, admirable qualities in a woman.

There are two other texts of note that were used in boarding houses. These are Hannah Milcah Hill Moore's 1796 *Miscellanies, Moral and Instructive, in Prose and Verse; Collected from Various Authors: for the Use of Schools, and Improvement of Young Persons of Both Sexes*,[38] and Priscilla Wakefield's 1799 *Mental Improvement or the Beauties and Wonders of Nature and Art in a Series of Instructive Conversations*.[39] These are not textbooks, but collections of quotations, poetry, and prose gleaned from classical literature, philosophy, and history books that would have been in textbooks for their male counterparts. Like today's journal or scrapbook, they represent the appreciation for erudite insights but remain acceptable because they do not offer the same linear instruction in these areas that was offered to men.

34. Ibid., 75.

35. Ibid., 80.

36. Ibid., 87.

37. Ibid., 96.

38. Moore, *Miscellanies*. The earliest edition was published in 1787 and the author was usually referred to as Milcah Martha Moore. The edition used in this book is the 1796 edition with the author's name as shown.

39. Wakefield, *Mental Improvement*. The earliest edition was published in 1794, with the U.S. edition published in 1799.

The Rise of Seminaries and Academies

Thomas Woody claims that the term "academy" was preferred in the early years and "seminary" was preferred later.[40] Predating both the influence of the First Ladies and the rise of Republican Motherhood, the earliest female academy was operated by the Ursuline Sisters in New Orleans. It opened in 1727 and had around 170 boarding pupils by 1803. In 1742, Countess Benigna Zinzendorf opened the Bethlehem Female Seminary (later the Moravian College for Women). It moved from Germantown to Bethlehem, Pennsylvania in 1749 and saw over seven thousand students who hailed from New York, Maryland, New Jersey, Rhode Island, Connecticut, South Carolina, and even as far away as Nova Scotia and the islands of the West Indies.[41] If we were to imagine life here, then we should imagine an atmosphere filled with music. Apparently, it was a part of what made this school such a joyful place.[42]

Religion was key to bringing about social equality for women. On the "College History" page for Moravian College, they write:

> Since the Moravians considered every human soul a potential candidate for salvation, every human being had to be educated. Comenius wrote in 1632 that "not the children of the rich or of the powerful only, but of all alike, boys and girls, both noble and ignoble, rich and poor, in all cities and towns, villages and hamlets, should be sent to school." The Moravians therefore considered schools secondary in importance only to churches.[43]

While much has been made of the Quaker influence on the advancement of women, little has been said about the Moravian influence. Yet, this institution still operates today. It became coed in 1954.[44] Another school opened by the Moravians in the eighteenth century was Linden Hall, opened in 1794 in Lititz, Pennsylvania.[45]

Other female academies that opened in the eighteenth century include two schools opened in New Haven. In 1780, a school was opened by William Woodbridge and in 1783 a school was opened by Jedediah Morse.

40. Woody, *A History of Women's Education*, 1:329.

41. Ibid., 1:330.

42. Ibid., 1:333.

43. Moravian College, "College History."

44. Ibid.

45. Woody, *A History of Women's Education*, 1:338, 340.

In 1784 Bingham's School for Girls opened in Boston, in 1785 Dwight's opened in Greenfield, and in 1789 a female academy opened in Medford.[46] In 1799, the Friends (Quakers) opened a school for girls in Westtown. One important addition to this list is Clinton Academy in East Hampton, New York. The first "First Lady" to receive a formal education was Anna Tuthill Symmes Harrison. She learned about the classics while she attended Clinton Academy, beginning in 1781. After that, she went to the boarding school of Isabella Marshal Graham from 1787–1791 in New York City.[47]

Also of note is the Academy for Females of Philadelphia that was opened by John Poor in 1787.[48] Some of the female students there made passionate arguments for a woman's right to speak publicly.[49] It was also the first to be incorporated. Woody dates that to 1792.[50] There, girls studied "reading, writing, arithmetic, English Grammar, composition, rhetoric, and geography."[51] Girls were allowed to learn "English, Latin, Greek, writing, arithmetic, speaking, geometry, logic, geography, or music" at the boys and girls school at Leicester, opened in 1784.[52] Many historians note Litchfield Academy, opened by Sarah Pierce in 1792. It began in her home, but did not stay there long.[53] In its forty years of operation (it closed in 1833), around 3,000 girls were educated there, according to the Litchfield Historical Society website.[54] Pierce organized girls to raise money for missionaries and ministers who needed to be trained. She engaged them in "moral reform movements" and "spread the ideals of Christianity, morality, education, and character" to their families and communities. Two of her students were Catharine Beecher and Harriet Beecher Stowe. Many of her students went onto become trained as teachers. Pierce understood the challenges of her time. Instead of having girls avoid subjects like botany and chemistry, she had them embroider or paint subjects related to science, literature, history,

46. Ibid.
47. National First Ladies' Library, "First Ladies Research."
48. Woody, *A History of Women's Education*, 1:333.
49. Ibid., 1:338.
50. Ibid., 1:337.
51. Ibid., 1:333.
52. Ibid., 1:340.
53. Ibid., 1:340.
54. Litchfield Historical Society, "A History."

and geography.[55] By doing so, she was able to educate them while engaging them in an activity considered appropriate at the time.

Education in the Nineteenth Century: "From Butterflies to Eagles"

Elevated to a new status of "Mothers of the Republic," as exemplified by their accomplished First Ladies, American women argued that they needed an education to understand and play out their new political roles in the home in the nineteenth century.[56] Thus, the academy and seminary began to replace boarding houses for girls, although many opened during the same time period in which they proliferated.[57] To exemplify the ideological turn that was a part of the turn, Horowitz's claimed their "sons now imbibed the milk of citizenship and virtue," so a more serious approach to education was needed.[58] Female academies and seminaries sprang up in response to this new need as well as in response to society's desire that women should be prepared to be excellent wives and mothers, and in both the eighteenth and nineteenth centuries emerging institutions were often designed and operated by women.[59] Not only did this create a turning point for women in terms of education, but the need for schools created a need for teachers. This in turn empowered women by offering them a legitimate profession outside of the home.[60]

In the nineteenth century, a visitor to a women's school in Ohio wrote:

> One word only in regard to your institution. Everything indicates that you have been well and faithfully trained not only to perform regularly certain exercises, but to think and acquaint yourselves with history. You cannot but know, then, that in all ages and in all countries, up to a very recent period, your half (and the common parlance is equally complimentary and true) the better half of the species was viewed, as a race holding to man the relation of butterflies to eagles. Cast by the beneficence of Providence in a more delicate mould, you were considered in the light of statues, in

---

55. Ibid.
56. Horowitz, *Alma Mater*, 10.
57. "Academies and Seminaries."
58. Horowitz, *Alma Mater*, 11.
59. Ibid., 329.
60. Ibid., 10–11.

which grace and beauty were the chief requisites, gaudy playthings in which mind was by no means necessary.

All that has passed away, and we hope, forever. A new era has dawned up you, not the mental deliverance and independence of Miss Frances Wright, separating you from God and eternity, as it would emancipate you from this base thralldom of the past. But it has been proved, no longer to be contested, that you have minds capable of illimitable progress, differing, indeed in some respects, from the male mind, but differing, perhaps in your favor. It has been shown, in innumerable instances, that you are quite as susceptible of intellectual, and more docile to moral training that man; that thus you can become, what you were formed to be, an helpmate for him, his intellectual companion, his guide, philosopher, and friend, cheering existence with a mental radiance all your own, a mental radiance differing from that of many, only by that beautiful diversity, which marks all the works of God.[61]

With Christian principles being used to justify education, the number of academies and seminaries proliferated. In fact, the scholar most known for work in this area, Thomas Woody, admits that there are really too many female academies and seminaries to list for the nineteenth century. Part of the problem is that so many opened for such a brief period of time. However, three are often used to characterize the whole era: Emma Willard and Troy Female Seminary (established 1821), Catharine Beecher and Hartford Female Seminary (established 1823), and Mary Lyon and Mount Holyoke Female Seminary (established 1837). Horowitz would add Zilpah Grant's in Ipswich, Massachusetts (1828) to the list because of its profound influence.[62] Later, the "Seven Sisters" would come to represent the best of female education, with only one of the original three still a part of the group. These are: Barnard College, Bryn Mawr College (founded by Quakers),[63] Mount Holyoke College, Radcliffe College, Smith College, Vassar College, and Wellesley College. "The Seven Sisters College Conference began in 1926," giving these institutions their nickname.[64]

All three women who founded the most famous female seminaries of the nineteenth century were devoted to Christ and made it a focus for the kind of education received at these institutions. According to the

61. Woody, *A History of Women's Education*, 1:369.

62. Horowitz, *Alma Mater*, 11.

63. Ibid., 6.

64. Ibid., xxii.

Encyclopedia of Modern Christian Politics, in response to the idea that a woman's highest goal is to please a man, Emma Willard once wrote that for a Christian "the will of God . . . is the only standard for perfection."[65] Mary Lyon was converted to Christianity by Joseph Emerson and ended up converting about 25 percent of her students over the course of her career.[66] She was, in effect, a woman minister of sorts.[67] Woody writes that,

> though religion played a prominent role in the life of most schools of the early part of the last century, and Christian character and usefulness were almost without exception reckoned as true objectives . . . there is no exaggeration in saying that at Mount Holyoke there was probably more personal religious fervor than in any other single institution. Miss Lyon was prone to regard the success of her efforts to create the school as sealing a covenant with God for the advancement of His Kingdom.[68]

Catharine Beecher was certainly no exception. Her famous essay, "American Women, Will You Save Your Country?" argued that women should work to convert people in the West.[69] On the University of Michigan's "Religion in Schools" webpage, they write:

> Evangelism was a significant cultural force during the first half of the nineteenth century and schools provided centers for revivals. Ministers preached and prayed over women students hoping the students would be converted; and some students came to school expecting and hoping for religious experiences.
>
> Because of the close association between seminaries and revivals, almost every denomination built their own seminaries and colleges where revivals were led by ministers from their own denomination. These schools were open to students from any religious persuasion, but attendance at weekly religious services and daily prayers were mandatory.[70]

Furthermore, the divide between "religion" and "science" was not much of a factor, they argue. In fact, women loved science and the curriculum

---

65. Domenico and Hanley, *Encyclopedia of Modern Christian Politics,* 594.

66. Woody, *A History of Women's Education,* 1:358.

67. Horowitz, *Alma Mater,* 16.

68. Woody, *A History of Women's Education,* 1:362.

69. Ibid., 1:363.

70. "Religion, Race, and Culture; Religion in Schools."

accommodated their interests in this area.[71] Historian Helen Horowitz describes the carryover of religion into women's colleges with critics stating that they were little more than "Protestant nunneries," though she goes on to illustrate this is far from the truth.[72]

First Lady Sarah Childress Polk (1803–1891)

Politics? Education? Religion? Of all the First Ladies, Sarah Polk is the best example of how a woman might navigate her position in society with strength and intelligence during the heart of the era when the female academy and seminary flourished. A devout Christian from a well-to-do family, Sarah was educated at one of the best female institutions of the time, the Moravian's academy at Salem, North Carolina.[73] At the Moravian Female Academy, she learned "Greek and Roman literature, grammar, writing techniques, world history, and home economics."[74] Before that, she went to Murfreesboro Common School in Murfreesboro, Tennessee from about 1808 to 1813 where learned "reading, writing and arithmetic." Next, she went to Bradley Academy in Murfreesboro, Tennessee for about two years between 1814 and 1816. It was actually a boys' school, but she and her sister were privately tutored there. Next, she went to Abercrombie's Boarding School in Nashville, Tennessee for about a year in 1816 to 1817. As the "First Ladies" website notes, "More of a finishing school of young women, here Sarah Childress Polk learned to play the piano, sewing and social etiquette."[75]

After her father's death, she inherited part of his estate, becoming wealthy before she was married.[76] She married a protégé of Andrew Jackson, James Polk, on New Years' Day in 1824 when she was only twenty years old.[77] He was of gentility, just as she was, and educated at the University of North Carolina as a lawyer, passing the bar in 1820.[78] He would serve as our eleventh President, from 1845 to 1849. She is said to have "exerted

---

71. Ibid.
72. Horowitz, *Alma Mater*, 4.
73. The White House, "Our First Ladies."
74. Ibid., Watson, 85.
75. Ibid., National First Ladies' Library, "First Ladies Research."
76. Watson, *American First Ladies*, 85.
77. The White House, "Our First Ladies."
78. Watson, *American First Ladies*, 85.

considerable influence on public affairs and politics" in her time.[79] Indeed, as "one of the most politically minded of the first ladies," and she assisted her husband with political activities and worked alongside him during his presidency without ever taking a vacation during the entire four years.[80]

On the "Our First Ladies" page of the White House website, it says:

> In an age when motherhood gave a woman her only acknowledged career, Sarah Polk had to resign herself to childlessness. Moreover, no lady would admit to a political role of her own, but Mrs. Polk found scope for her astute mind as well as her social skills. She accompanied her husband to Washington whenever she could, and they soon won a place in its most select social circles. Constantly—but privately—Sarah was helping him with his speeches, copying his correspondence, giving him advice. Much as she enjoyed politics, she would warn him against overwork. He would hand her a newspaper "Sarah, here is something I wish you to read . . ."—and she would set to work as well.[81]

Another source states:

> She [Sarah] quickly came to share her husband's political ambitions, becoming (in the judgment of one historian) his "most valuable political ally." During James's tenure in the House of Representatives (1825–39), which included four years as speaker (1835–39), Sarah usually accompanied him to Washington, D.C., where she was a popular hostess and noted conversationalist. Although she could not travel with him on his campaigns because it would have been considered inappropriate, she sent him documents and kept him apprised of the local political scene.[82]

Sarah Polk is an example of how women were still cleverly negotiating societal limitations to participate in political society long before twentieth-century women would do so as equals. Watson notes that the Polks spent fourteen years in the "highest social and political circles of Washington" as he served in Congress, including as Speaker of the House.[83] Using her intellectual abilities to their fullest, she "read the newspapers of the day, at-

79. "Sarah Polk." in *Encyclopedia Britannica*: http://www.britannica.com/EBchecked/topic/710808/Sarah-Polk.

80. Robertson, "Biographies of the First Ladies," 162–63.

81. Mrs. Polk was in many ways like Aspasia, the wife of the Greek leader Pericles.

82. "Sarah Polk." in *Encyclopedia Britannica*: http://www.britannica.com/EBchecked/topic/710808/Sarah-Polk.

83. Watson, *American First Ladies*, 86.

tended sessions of the legislature, became knowledgeable of significant bills and their process of passage, and discussed politics at a very high level."[84] In addition to answering her husband's mail and writing some of his speeches, she campaigned for philanthropic projects, like building the Washington Monument.[85] Her husband had her collect and present news articles each day with what he should read, guiding his attention to the political and social causes of most interest to her. Realizing her influence and respecting her knowledge, civic leaders in Washington "sought her political counsel" as well as her husband's.[86]

Many professional women today actively seek a mentor. Sarah did the same, drawing on the wisdom of Dolley Madison, who was in her late seventies when Sarah became First Lady at the age of forty-one.[87] She was known for being an expert at maintaining decorum, refusing to serve hard liquor in the White House ("Sahara Sarah"), to host dances, to attend card parties, or to attend horse races.[88] Contemporary scholars who focus on recovering women's history know just how powerful seemingly benign parties were, especially tea parties. Attending these with Dolley, she probably influenced women and their husbands in countless ways during her time.[89]

Sarah is also an example of the business acumen women possess, despite societal limitations. After her husband's death, she ran their Mississippi cotton plantation very profitably for the next eleven years.[90] Unlike many other First Ladies, Sarah did not have to beg the White House for a pension, although she did receive one after a bill passed in 1882 granting all living widows of presidents a pension.[91] She retired comfortably at Polk Place in Nashville, where she died in 1891, thirty years after selling the plantation.[92] Of course, she is also known for having owned slaves, both in the White House and later.[93] More importantly, her business acumen was

84. Ibid.

85. Ibid.

86. Ibid., 87.

87. Ibid.

88. Ibid., 87–88.

89. Ibid., 87.

90. Robertson, "Biographies of the First Ladies," 163; Watson, *American First Ladies*, 85.

91. Watson, *American First Ladies*, 90.

92. Robertson, "Biographies of the First Ladies," 163.

93. Watson, *American First Ladies*, 362. He notes that Martha Washington and Margaret Taylor also owned slaves.

clear when she argued that a National Bank should be established—a view opposite that of her husband's.[94] Polk did created an independent treasury in 1846 while he was President, but it would be 1863 before a National Bank Act would be passed and 1913 before the creation of the Federal Reserve.[95]

To sum up, in many ways Sarah Polk is one illustration of the central premise of this book—that education led to the rise of social justice for women. Watson notes that "Sarah established a basis for a woman to participate fully in political debates, exchange views, and contribute her own agenda and style" in a time that required she still do so under the auspices of her husband's career. Receiving the best education she could procure, she was "well educated, well versed on current issues," and determined that her husband would succeed.[96] She was, in many ways, an exemplification of the ironies embodied by the women of her time. Strong, educated, and intelligent, she wielded her social intelligence with skill and ease, accomplishing her political and social goals while maintaining her place in society.

First Ladies of the White House: Entering the Academy or Seminary

Other First Ladies enjoyed similar types of educational opportunities that Mrs. Polk enjoyed. Julia Gardiner Tyler attended the Madame N. D. Chagaray Institute for Young Ladies from April 1835 to December 1837 and perhaps again in January through December of 1848 in New York City. It was "a finishing school for the daughters of elite New York families, with a curriculum of music, French literature, ancient history, arithmetic, and composition." Before then, she probably received private tutoring at home in New York.[97] Eliza McCardle Johnson attended Rhea Academy in Greeneville, Tennessee sometime between 1816 and 1823. "Among the classes available to Eliza McCardle were those in reading, spelling, writing, English, grammar, arithmetic, geography, composition, needlework, history, philosophy and, importantly, rhetoric."[98]

Frances Cleveland first attended Madame Brecker's French Kindergarten from 1870–1871 in Buffalo, New York, then Miss Bissell's School

94. Ibid., 89.

95. Ibid.

96. Ibid., 90.

97. National First Ladies' Library, "First Ladies Research."

98. Ibid.

for Young Ladies, then the Medina Academy for Boys and Girls, in Medina, New York, then Central [High] School, Buffalo, New York from 1879 to 1881 and last to Wells College in Aurora, New York from 1882 to1885 where she "successfully passed exams in Latin and German to gain entrance in the winter semester at one of the first U.S. liberal arts colleges for women," and where "she developed her avocation for photography at this time but also studied academic subjects that further included botany, astronomy, logic, religious studies, and she especially enjoyed political science. She was active in the theater club, building sets, sewing costumes and acting. She was also a member of the Phoenix Society, a debating club, once delivering a complicated speech on free trade, the tariff and protectionism." Ida Saxton McKinley attended Miss Sanford's School, Cleveland, Ohio and Brooke Hall Female Seminary in Media, Pennsylvania.[99]

Edith Kermit Carow Roosevelt first learned at home, then at the Dodsworth School for Dancing and Deportment in New York (1869–1871), and then the Louise Comstock Private School in New York from 1871 to 1879. "Under the influence of the disciplinarian headmistress, Edith Carow developed a highly moralistic and religious sensibility which forever marked her character. She excelled in writing and developed a lifelong love of Shakespeare. Among the subjects she studied were English History, English Literature, Latin, German, French, zoology, botany, physiology, elemental arithmetic, philosophy, penmanship, singing, and music appreciation. With fellow students, she attended symphony concerts, choral performances, the theater, the circus, and military review drills."[100]

Helen Louise Heron Taft attended the Miss Nourse School in Cincinnati, Ohio from 1866–1879 and learned "history, mythology and elemental science, along with the basics of reading, writing and arithmetic. During these years, her lifelong love of music was also borne out of lessons from George Schneider from the Cincinnati Music School, who taught at the Nourse School. When she was eleven years old, Nellie Herron entered the "high department" and was additionally taught English literature, two branches of natural sciences, French, German, Latin and Greek." She then attended the University of Cincinnati in 1881 and studied German and chemistry.[101]

First Lady Ellen Louise Axson Wilson learned at home then at a "local female college" in Georgia. Later, First Lady Edith Bolling Galt Wilson

99. Ibid.
100. Ibid.
101. Ibid.

went to Martha Washington College in Abingdon, Virginia for about a year in 1877 and 1878, and then went to The Richmond Female Seminary (aka Powell's School) in 1889 and 1890 in Richmond, Virginia. Florence Harding went to the Union School in Marion, Ohio from 1866–1876. There, "she was instructed by both male and female teachers in math, science, English, writing, surveying, rhetoric, logic, philosophy, history, geography, Latin, Greek, German, cartology, and astronomy." After that, she went to the Cincinnati Conservatory of Music from 1877 to1878 and wanted "to become an internationally-recognized concert pianist."[102]

Finally, Elizabeth Truman only went to high school at Independence High School, Independence, Missouri, 1898–1901, First Lady Bess Wallace, a skilled tennis player, graduated from Miss Barstow's School in Kansas City after two years of school (1901–1903), and Mamie Eisenhower went to the Miss Wolcott School for Girls from 1914 to 1915 in Denver, Colorado and Miss Hayden's Dance School.[103]

Conclusion

To conclude, we are indebted to many of the women who feminists today would not define as supporters for women's equality, but who should be acknowledged for their influence, such as the First Ladies of the White House. These women, who all the while appeared to acquiesce to the political, social, and religious restrictions placed upon women in eighteenth and nineteenth-century America, lived lives pursuing ambitious educational, political, social, and religious bids for equality that were evidence of their true leanings. Using whatever level of education they had, the First Ladies influenced men and women in the highest levels of government. Their influence on the rise of equality for women is clear, despite any lip service they gave to the social mores of the day.

102. Ibid.
103. Ibid.

4

Selected List of Female Academies and Seminaries

Selected List of Female Seminaries and Academies Opened in the Eighteenth and Nineteenth Centuries

WHAT FOLLOWS IS A list of many of the female seminaries and academies opened in the eighteenth and nineteenth centuries. Many of these schools are named for Thomas Jefferson's famous home, Monticello. This breathtaking residence (although smaller than one might expect) perhaps represented an idyllic location as well as the kind of intellectual fervor and breadth of curiosity represented by Jefferson himself that many admired. Some are named for George Washington (a great proponent of education), some for the religious organizations that founded them, some for the individuals who either founded them or funded them, and a vast majority are simply named for their geographical location. The height of the female seminary's popularity was between about 1830 and 1860, with Virginia creating several in the 1890s more as secondary schools then as a replacement for college.[1] Before 1820, boys' schools flourished and were "encouraged by legislatures," but girls' schools were few.[2] One final note is that several schools begun by the Five Civilized Tribes have been included in this list. The list includes the schools opened in Oklahoma, but prior to its statehood in 1907, Oklahoma was known as Indian Territory.

1. Woody, *A History of Women's Education*, 1:391, 393.
2. Ibid., 1:394.

- 1727, The earliest female academy in what would become the United States was operated by the Ursuline Sisters in New Orleans.
- 1742, Countess Benigna Zinzendorf opened the Bethlehem Female Seminary (later the Moravian College for Women). It moved from Germantown to Bethlehem, Pennsylvania in 1749.
- 1780, a school was opened by William Woodbridge.
- 1783, a school was opened by Jedediah Morse.
- 1784, Bingham's School for Girls opened in Boston.
- 1785, Dwight's opened in Greenfield.
- 1787, the Academy for Females of Philadelphia was opened by John Poor in 1787.
- 1789, a female academy opened in Medford.[3]
- 1792, Litchfield Academy, opened by Sarah Pierce.
- 1799, the Friends (Quakers) opened a school for girls in Westtown.
- 1802, The first exclusively female academy opened in the nineteenth century, by the Moravians, Salem, North Carolina.[4] Presidential First Lady Sarah Whitsett Childress Polk attended it in 1818–1820. There, she learned "English grammar, Bible study, Greek and Roman literature, geography, music, drawing, and sewing."
- 1803, Bradford in New Bedford, Massachusetts.[5]
- 1806, John Lyle's Female Seminary, Kentucky.[6]
- 1806, Moses Fisk's Female Academy, Hilham, Tennessee, and Liberty Academy in Springfield, Tennessee.[7]
- 1807, Ann Smith Academy in Lexington, Virginia.[8]
- 1807, Pittsfield, Massachusetts.
- 1808, Bath Female Academy, Massachusetts.

3. Ibid., 1:338.
4. Ibid., 1:341.
5. Ibid., 1:342.
6. Ibid., 1:384.
7. Ibid.; Reid and Gregory, *Robertson County, Tennessee*, 43.
8. Woody, *A History of Women's Education*, 1:391.

- 1808, Nazareth Academy, Bardstown, Kentucky.[9]
- 1808, Richmond Female Academy, Virginia.[10]
- 1809, Baltimore Female Academy, Maryland (supported by a lottery).[11]
- 1811, Knoxville Female Academy, Tennessee.[12]
- 1812, Friends' Academy, New Bedford, Massachusetts.
- 1812, Portland, Maine, school for girls opened by Martin Ruter.[13]
- 1813, Maryville Female Academy, Tennessee.[14]
- 1814, Ursuline Convent for the education of girls, New York.[15]
- 1814–1837, Catherine Fiske at Keene, New Hampshire; educated over 2500 girls. She adopted a popular maxim of the time: It was a "man's office to correct evil and a woman's to prevent it."[16]
- 1817, Nashville Female Academy, Tennessee.[17]
- 1818, New Glasgow Female Academy, Virginia.[18]
- 1818–1824, Joseph Emerson's Ladies' Seminary at Byfield, then Saugus, then Wethersfield in Connecticut; Mary Lyon and Zilpah Grant were his students.[19]
- 1818, Bangor Young Ladies' Academy.[20]
- 1818, Madame Perdreville's school for girls, Missouri.[21]
- 1819, Mrs. Love's School for Young Ladies, Franklin, Missouri.

9. Ibid., 1:384.
10. Ibid., 392.
11. Ibid., 1:390.
12. Ibid., 1:384.
13. Ibid., 1:364.
14. Ibid., 1:384.
15. Ibid., 1:365.
16. Ibid., 1:343.
17. Ibid., 1:384.
18. Ibid., 1:392.
19. Ibid., 1:344.
20. Ibid., 1:165.
21. Ibid., 1:379.

- 1819, Brainerd Mission, Chattanooga, Tennessee. School for Cherokees.[22]

- 1819, Madison and Washington Academies, Illinois.[23]

- 1819, Elizabeth Female Academy, Mississippi, established by Elizabeth Roach and overseen by the Methodist Conference. It was the first institution for girls after Mississippi was admitted to the Union.[24]

- 1821, Troy Seminary, established by Emma Willard; said to "mark the beginning of higher education for women in the United States."[25]

- 1821, Lafayette Seminary, Lexington, Kentucky.[26]

- 1821, The University of Alabama selects a "site for a female institution," and in 1822, section 17 of the Act is added and states that the institution must create "three branches of said University for Female Education."[27]

- 1822, Athens Female Academy, Alabama.[28]

- 1823, The St. Louis Female Academy, Missouri.[29]

- 1823, The Adams Academy in Derry, New Hampshire (first to be endowed exclusively for girls with a bequest from Jacob Adams). Zilpah Grant took charge in 1824 and "transformed" it into a "first class school." Mary Lyon worked there with her in the summers until 1828 until both of them left, along with several students.[30]

- 1823, George B. Emerson's private secondary school, Boston.[31] Convinced by William Sullivan, he opened this school to much success.[32] In 1831, Emerson addressed the American Institute of Instruction, arguing for women's education.

22. Mihesuah, *Cultivating the Rosebuds*, 8.
23. Woody, *A History of Women's Education*, 1:371.
24. Ibid., 1:382–83.
25. Ibid., 1:344.
26. Ibid., 1:384.
27. Ibid., 1:388.
28. Ibid.
29. Ibid., 1:379.
30. Ibid., 1:348.
31. Ibid., 1:343.
32. Ibid., 1:347–49.

- 1823, Hartford Female Seminary, Catharine Beecher (sister of Harriet Beecher Stowe, author of *Uncle Tom's Cabin*, the most influential anti-slavery book of its time); She wrote, "The amount of intellectual activity and the delightful enthusiasm of interest that prevailed so universally, both among teachers and pupils, . . . exceeded anything of which I had ever known."[33]

- 1824, Harmony Grove Female Academy, Georgia.[34]

- 1825, The Washington School for Young Ladies at Franklin, Missouri.[35]

- 1825, Science Hill, Kentucky.[36]

- 1826, Danville Female Academy, Virginia.[37]

- 1826, Tuscambria Female Academy, Alabama.[38]

- 1826, Mrs. Pierce's School in Fayette, Bethlehem Monastery Female School in Perry County, Paris Female Seminary, and Miss Willard's Seminary for Young Ladies, Missouri.[39]

- 1827, Monroe Academy, Illinois.[40]

- 1827, Shelby Female Academy, Lexington, Kentucky. It was also called Ward's Academy, after its director. First Lady Mary Todd Lincoln attended for about ten years, from 1827 to 1837, with a year off for a visit to Springfield.[41]

- 1828, Ipswich Female Seminary; Zilpah Grant and Mary Lyon worked there together from 1828–1835 until Grant left. They made it a top school in its time.[42] It trained teachers who took over schools in Ohio, Indiana, Illinois, Iowa, and Wisconsin.[43]

33. Ibid., 1:354.
34. Ibid., 1:387.
35. Ibid., 1:379.
36. Ibid., 1:384.
37. Ibid., 1:392.
38. Ibid., 1:388.
39. Ibid., 1:379.
40. Ibid., 1:371.
41. Baker, *Mary Todd Lincoln*, 34, 37.
42. Woody, *A History of Women's Education*, 1:350.
43. Ibid., 1:352.

- 1829, Sparta Female Seminary, Talbotton Female Seminary, and Monroe Female Seminary, Georgia.[44]

- 1829, Abbot Female Academy, Andover, Massachusetts; financially supported by Sarah Abbott with gifts of over ten thousand dollars and run by men until 1853. This is when Miss Hasseltine took over and began awarding diplomas.[45] The school was devoted to training women to become teachers.

- 1829, Hallowell, Maine, incorporated in 1791, begins to educate girls in 1829.[46]

- 1830, Kalorama Seminary (later the Virginia Female Institute), Virginia.[47]

- 1830, Cambridge Female Academy, Maryland.[48]

- 1830, Sims Female Academy, Alabama.[49]

- 1830, Maine Wesleyan Seminary, Kent's Hill, begins to admit girls in 1830, shortly after its establishment.[50]

- 1831, Academy at Waterville, Maine, begins to admit female students.[51]

- 1831, Tuscaloosa Female Academy and Huntsville Female Seminary (for the latter, the principal was a teacher trained by Catharine Beecher), Alabama.[52]

- 1832, Wheelock Academy, later known as the Wheelock Female Seminary, was built and used as a model school for Choctaws in Oklahoma. In 1842, it became the first Choctaw National Academy and other tribes used it as a model as well. It closed in 1861, as all Choctaw schools did, because of the Civil War.[53]

44. Ibid., 1:387.

45. Ibid., 1:357.

46. Ibid., 1:364.

47. Ibid., 1:392.

48. Ibid., 1:390.

49. Ibid., 1:388.

50. Ibid., 1:364.

51. Ibid.

52. Ibid., 1:388.

53. See "Wheelock Academy," http://www.okgenweb.org/schools/county/choctaw-nat/wheelock.htm.

- 1833, Boonsborough Seminary, Maryland.[54]

- 1833 (incorporated), Newton County Female Seminary and LaGrange Female Academy, Georgia.[55]

- 1833, Chillicothe Female Seminary, Ohio.[56] The first to graduate with a degree, First Lady Lucy Ware Webb Hayes began at the Miss Baskerville School before going to the Chillicothe Female School in Chillicothe, Ohio from about 1837 to 1844. From 1844 to 1847, she went to the Ohio Wesleyan Preparatory Department in Delaware, Ohio and learned "French, composition, grammar, and penmanship." From 1847 to 1850, she attended Cincinnati Wesleyan Female College and studied "rhetoric, geometry, geology, astronomy, trigonometry, mental and moral science, German, French, drawing, painting, music." She earned her college degree at Wesleyan Female College. Her graduation speech topic was "The Influence of Christianity on National Prosperity."[57] Her political influence is widely noted, and is described "as being the embodiment of the New Woman," i.e., one who wanted to enter the workplace and politics.[58] By becoming the president of the Women's Home Missionary Society, she was able to enter the political realm without drawing criticism.[59]

- 1833, Detroit Female Seminary, Rese's High School for Young Ladies, and St. Clare's Seminary for Ladies, Michigan. The Detroit Female Seminary was run by Miss Tappan and Miss Nichols.[60]

- 1833, Female Seminary, Monroe County, Bloomington, Indiana. Also, Washington County Seminary which focused on educating women to be teachers.[61]

- 1834, Patapsco Female Institute, Maryland.[62]

54. Ibid., 1:390.
55. Ibid., 1:387.
56. Ibid., 1:367.
57. National First Ladies' Library, "First Ladies Research."
58. Watson, *American First Ladies*, 363.
59. Ibid., 363.
60. Woody, *A History of Women's Education*, 1:370.
61. Ibid., 1:371.
62. Ibid., 1:390–91.

- 1834, Culloden Female Academy, Georgia.[63]

- 1835, Forsyth Female Academy, Georgia.

- 1835, Granville, Western, and Circleville Female Seminaries, Ohio. The Western Female Institute was run by Misses Dutton and Tappan but started by Catharine Beecher and her sister, Harriet Beecher Stowe.[64]

- 1835, Alabama Female Institute.[65]

- 1835, Jacksonville Female Academy, Illinois. Opened in 1833 under Sarah Crocker (who was recommended by Mary Lyon), and later run by Emily P. Price (recommended by Zilpah Grant). Woody points out this important detail: "It was here that the Ladies' Educational Society was formed, having as its principal object the preparation of young women for teaching."[66]

- 1835, Georgetown Female Academy and Georgetown Female Seminary, both opened by Dr. J. E. Farnham, Kentucky.[67]

- 1835, Elias Marks Female Academy at Barhamsville, Columbia, Yorkville, Barnwell, and Pendleton Female Academies, and Presbyterian Female Seminary in Anderson, South Carolina.[68]

- 1836, Clarkesville and Lynchburg Female Academies, Virginia.[69]

- 1836, Rockville Female Seminary, Maryland.[70]

- 1836, Monticello Female Academy, Georgia.[71]

- 1837, West Point Female Academy, Georgia.[72]

- 1837, Mount Holyoke Female Seminary; run by Mary Lyon until her death in 1849.

63. Ibid., 1:387.
64. Ibid., 1:368.
65. Ibid., 1:390.
66. Ibid., 1:372.
67. Ibid., 1:384.
68. Ibid.
69. Ibid., 1:392.
70. Ibid., 1:390.
71. Ibid., 1:387.
72. Ibid.

- 1837, The Michigan legislature passed legislation providing for women's colleges and Marshall, Utica, Ann Arbor, and Oakland Female Seminaries opened. Also, opened were the Young Ladies' Seminary of Monroe City and the Michigan Female Seminary at Kalamazoo.[73]

- 1838, Hannah More Academy, Maryland.[74]

- 1838, Gainesville Female High School, Georgia.[75]

- 1838, Monticello Female Seminary, Illinois. Begun by Benjamin Godfrey who visited several schools in the east and consulted with Mary Lyon before hiring one of Zilpah Grant's teachers as the school's first principal.[76]

- 1838–1839, thirty-four different seminaries opened in Pennsylvania after an act was passed to fund them.[77]

- 1838, Norwalk Female Seminary, Ohio.[78]

- 1838, Columbia Female Institute, Tennessee.[79]

- 1839, Baltimore Academy of the Visitation, Maryland.[80]

- 1839, Judson Female Institute at Marion, Alabama.[81]

- 1839, New Hagerstown, Ravenna, Worthington Seminaries and Oxford Female Academy, Ohio. Oxford was founded by Bethania Crocker in 1830, it was incorporated in 1839, and it became a college in 1852.[82]

- 1839, Appling Female Academy, Georgia.[83]

- 1839, Clinton Female Institute, Georgia (merged with Georgia Female College).[84]

73. Ibid., 1:370.
74. Ibid., 1:391.
75. Ibid., 1:387.
76. Ibid., 1:372–73.
77. Ibid., 1:366.
78. Ibid., 1:367.
79. Ibid., 1:384.
80. Ibid., 1:391.
81. Ibid., 1:390.
82. Ibid., 1:367.
83. Ibid., 1:387.
84. Ibid.

- 1839, Farmville Female Seminary, Virginia.[85]

- 1840, Edgeworth Seminary, Greensboro, North Carolina.[86]

- 1840, St. Mary's County Female Seminary, Maryland.[87]

- 1841, Marion Female Academy and Seminary, Alabama.[88]

- 1841, Athens Female Academy, Ohio.[89]

- 1842, "Spencer Academy [not noted whether it was for boys or girls or both], Fort Coffee Academy, Koonaha (Kunaha or Sunsha) Female Seminary, Ianubbee (Ayanubbe) Female Seminary, Chuwahla (Chuwalla) Female Seminary, and Wheelock Female Seminary. Fort Coffee Academy was divided into a male and a female branch in 1845. The latter, located five miles southeast of Fort Coffee, was called New Hope Seminary."[90] These schools were opened in Indian Territory (Oklahoma).

- 1842, Mary Baldwin Female Seminary, Staunton, Virginia.[91]

- 1842, Frederick Female Seminary, Maryland.[92]

- 1843, Methodist Episcopal Female Institute, Alabama (called the Athens College for Women from 1889 onward).[93]

- 1843, Oakland Female Seminary, Methodist Female Collegiate Institute, and St. Mary's Female Educational Institute, Ohio.[94]

- 1843, Geauga Seminary, Chester, Ohio.[95] First Lady Lucretia Rudolph Garfield went to Garrettsville Public Grammar School from 1838 to 1847 in Garrettsville, Ohio, then to Geauga Seminary in Ohio for two years and learned "Greek and Latin, and also included algebra, science, geography and music." Next, she went to the Hiram Eclectic

85. See http://www.markerhistory.com/longwood-university-marker-i-15-a/.
86. Ibid., 1:383.
87. Ibid., 1:391.
88. Ibid., 1:390.
89. Ibid., 1:372.
90. Miles, "Choctaw Boarding Schools."
91. Woody, *A History of Women's Education*, 1:392.
92. Ibid., 1:391.
93. Ibid., 1:390.
94. Ibid., 1:372.
95. Geiger, *History of Higher Education Annual*, 61.

Institute for five years from 1850 to 1855. This was also in Ohio. She continued her study of Greek and Latin, classical literature, British literature, and French literature. "She helped to organize a literary society which staged elocution, debate and oratorical presentations, often taking to the stage herself and defending the rights of women to do so at a time when many men considered it improper for women to so publicly present themselves. She also worked as editor and illustrator of *The Eclectic Star*, a school magazine."[96]

- 1845, Cooper Female Academy, Ohio.[97]
- 1846, Cherokee National Female Seminary, Oklahoma.[98]
- 1847, Illinois Conference Female Seminary and Rockford Female Seminary. Rockford was the idea of a conference of churches.[99]
- 1847, Lagrange Female Institute, Georgia.[100]
- 1848, Oak Ridge Mission, Seminole school for boys and girls in Oklahoma.[101]
- 1848, Springfield Female Academy, Tennessee.[102]
- 1848, Felicity Female Seminary, Ohio.
- 1849, Springfield Female Seminary, Oxford Female Institute, and Mansfield Female Seminary, Ohio.[103] First Lady Caroline Levinia Scott Harrison's father, a science and math professor, opened the Oxford Female Institute in Oxford, Ohio in 1849. "At the Institute, Caroline mastered English literature, for which she developed a lifelong love, drama, music, art and painting. She graduated in 1853 with a degree in music. She taught music, home economics and painting, both in Oxford and in Kentucky. She loved painting, first watercolors and then china painting, and she painted for her entire life."[104]

96. National First Ladies' Library, "First Ladies Research."
97. Woody, *A History of Women's Education*, 1:372.
98. Faulk and Welge, *Oklahoma*, 108.
99. Woody, *A History of Women's Education*, 1:372, 374.
100. Ibid., 1:387.
101. Frank, "Seminole."
102. Reid and Gregory, *Robertson County, Tennessee*, 43.
103. Woody, *A History of Women's Education*, 1:367.
104. National First Ladies' Library, "First Ladies Research."

- 1849, Oread Collegiate Institute, Worcester, Massachusetts; established by Eli Thayer and housed in a building much like a castle.[105]

- 1849, Lagrange Female College, Georgia.[106]

- 1850, Baltimore Female College, Maryland.[107]

- 1850, Defiance, Xenia, and Elliot Female Seminaries, Soeurs de Notre Dame Institute at Chillicothe, Ohio.

- 1850, Milwaukee Normal School and High School, helped by Catharine E. Beecher.[108]

- 1851, Cleveland, Sigourney, and Cody Female Seminaries, Ohio.[109]

- 1851, The Lexington College for Women, Missouri.[110]

- 1852, The Bloomfield Academy for Chickasaw Females, Oklahoma. Located on the Red River, across from Denison, Texas.[111]

- 1853, Female Seminary, Dubuque, Iowa; fostered by the newly formed American Women's Education Association, Catharine Beecher opened its doors in 1854.[112]

- 1853, New Orleans Female Collegiate Institute.[113]

- 1853, Baltimore Collegiate Institute, Maryland.[114]

- 1855, Mount Ida Female College, Davenport, Iowa.[115]

- 1856, Mount Washington Female College, Maryland.[116]

- 1859, Lyons Female College, Iowa.

- 1863, Mount Pleasant Female Seminary, Iowa.

---

105. Woody, *A History of Women's Education*, 1:362.

106. Ibid., 1:387.

107. Ibid., 1:391.

108. Ibid., 1:377.

109. Ibid., 1:367.

110. Ibid., 1:379.

111. Cobb, *Listening to our Grandmother's Stories*; Vaughn, "Douglas H. C. Johnston."

112. Woody, *A History of Women's Education*, 1:378.

113. Ibid.

114. Ibid., 1:391.

115. Ibid., 1:378.

116. Ibid., 1:391.

- 1864, St. Agatha's Seminary, Iowa City.[117]
- 1880, Sasakwa Female Academy, for the Seminole Tribe, Oklahoma.[118]
- 1890, Belmont Seminary at Liberty and Jeter Female Institute, Virginia.[119]
- 1891, Mekasukey Academy, accepted girls after 1911. Seminole Tribe, Oklahoma.[120]
- 1892, Ryland Institute, Blackstone Female Institute, and Virginia Christian Female Seminary, Virginia.
- 1894, Wartbury Seminary and Chatham Female Episcopal Institute, Virginia.
- 1894, Emahaka Mission, Seminole word meaning "girls' school," established in Oklahoma.[121]
- 1896, Newport News Female Seminary, Virginia.
- 1900, Rawlings Institute, Virginia.
- 1901, Hollins Institute and Sweet Briar Institute, Virginia.
- 1902, Bowling Green Female Seminary, Virginia.

117. Ibid., 1:378.
118. Koenig, "Seminole Schools."
119. Woody, *A History of Women's Education*, 1:378.
120. Koenig, "Seminole Schools."
121. Ibid.

5

An Evolving Curriculum

Case in Point: The Young Ladies Seminary

According to an early catalog of the Young Ladies Seminary (now Mills College of Oakland California, founded in 1852 in the city of Benicia, California), its curriculum was as follows:

> Course of Study. It is designed that the English course for those who are prepared to enter the Junior Class, shall occupy three years; but for those who study one or more languages, more time is required.
>
> Preparatory Class—Reading, Spelling, Writing, Geography, Grammar, Arithmetic (mental and written) and History of the United States.
>
> Junior Year—Arithmetic (completed), Algebra (begun), Book Keeping, Analysis of the English Language, Elements of Physiology, Elements of Moral Science, and History of England.
>
> Middle Year—Algebra (completed), Geometry (commenced), Botany, Philosophy and Universal History.
>
> Senior Year—Geometry (finished), Astronomy, Chemistry, Mental Philosophy, and Kames' Elements of Criticism.
>
> Studies—Optional.

Languages – Greek, Latin, French, Spanish, Italian, and German.

Fine Arts—Vocal Music, Instrumental (Piano and Guitar), Drawing, Reading, Compositions, and Calisthenics, pursued through the entire course.[1]

In terms of religious training, the catalog continues, "The school is entirely free from sectarianism in any form; but a wholesome moral influence will be exerted at all times, in regard to the manners and habits of the pupils. The young ladies are expected to attend church once on the Sabbath, regularly. The teachers will accompany them to such places of worship as they may choose to attend."[2]

The Young Ladies Seminary was founded in 1852 and by this year, the female seminary movement had reached the West Coast. At this point in our country's history, "American education was sailing full speed into an educational system where women were coming to be seen as the intellectual equals of men, possessing equal rights to a liberal education with a classical curriculum."[3] The female seminary had reached the apex of its importance to the development of women's education and would soon give way to the woman's college and normal schools (schools whose specific purpose was training teachers).

The curriculum of the Young Ladies' Seminary is representative of the evolution of the curricular profile that emerged in the schools that this movement produced and is a far cry from that of the "academy" founded by the Ursuline Sisters in 1727 which focused on "industrial training and religion." In order to understand the evolution of women's education in the United States, especially as it is reflected in female seminaries, it is important to understand changing perceptions of the mental capabilities of women and shifting perceptions of women's role within American society, both in terms of public/home sphere and of their moral influence on men. These have high impact on the opportunities and challenges women face in the classroom and the learning experiences to which they are exposed.

1. "Young Ladies' Seminary, Benicia," 6.
2. Ibid., 7–8.
3. Sweet, "Female Seminary," 41.

Education and the American Experience

The American experience begins with colonies that had a rural economy that was supported by port cities. Economically, barter was the main form of financial exchange and a cash economy has yet to evolve. Early education for white middle class females was framed within the context of domesticity and skills that made them better wives and mothers.

Concurrent with the framing of women's roles in society was a belief that women had lesser mental capacity than men and therefore unable to take on too rigorous a curriculum. Governor Winthrop of the Massachusetts Bay Colony believed that Mistress Hopkins, the wife of the governor of the Connecticut Colony, had gone insane from spending too much reading and writing. This was also the conclusion of Thomas Parker who wrote, "Her husband being very loving and tender to her, was loath to grieve her; but he saw his error, when it was too late. For if she had attended her household affairs and such things as belong to women, and not gone out of her way and calling to meddle in such things as are proper to men, whose minds are strong, etc., she had kept her wits, and might have improved them usefully and honorably in the place God had set her."[4]

Perceptions of women's religiosity and moral strength would also influence the purposes and curriculum of women's education. Historically, women have made up the majority of adherents in American faith-based groups and through their religious involvement; women formed an important part of their self-identity and in optimal circumstances, cohesion and a sense of networking with other women. Because women were increasingly viewed as the morally superior gender, education was important for their role in society, as an influence on both their children and on their husbands. With the advent of evangelicalism on the American scene through the First (1731–55) and Second Great Awakening (1790–1840), the requirement of public testimony of one's faith experience would be a training ground for women's move away from the home sphere and into the public sphere of teaching.

Through their experience with the Christian faith women would experience both a liberating and oppressive environment for their personal growth. "The Christian religion, as a multifarious ideology, has the ability to empower and to oppress simultaneously."[5] Evangelical theology posited an egalitarian perspective in regards to the salvation of men and women

---

4. Tucker and Liefeld, *Daughters of the Church*, 217.
5. Lindman, "Beyond the Meetinghouse," 153–54.

and their equal responsibility to share the Gospel and shape pietistic lives in accordance with their faith tradition. At the same time, within the organized church, specific Scriptures and examples of the Bible were and continue to be utilized by men to keep women in second tier status within their various denominations.

As the American experience begins during the colonial period, the paradigm of the "good wife" dominates. Thought to be mentally inferior to her spouse, the woman was to obey and serve her husband, nurture her children and maintain their household. Female subordination and domesticity were the benchmarks of a "good wife." Except among the Quakers where women could hold office and "exhort" (preach), women were restricted from roles in the public sphere of the church. This was also especially true in secular settings. Additionally, the Puritan ideal of a well-organized household also dominated society. However, regardless of this focus of early female education making "women better wives and mothers, virtually no school taught domestic economy, housewifery, or childrearing."[6]

The transition from the "good wife" of the colonial period to "Republican Motherhood" of the new nation occurs rather early in the American experiment. The ability of America to survive as a democratic society depended on a moral and intelligent citizenry. Who then, played the most central role in preparing the next generation of American citizens? Mothers—mothers who, with the appropriate education, could instill in their sons and daughters the virtues and intellectual skills necessary for succeeding generations to establish and grow a thriving republic. This paradigm provided the foundation for support of education of women.

There is a paradox in the thinking regarding women within the American experience. "As daughters of Eve, they were weak in faith and intellect,"[7] and yet women would become viewed as morally superior to men and intellectually capable to educate children in critical thinking and knowledge and skills necessary to become ideal citizens. "The role of Republican Mother was not simply imposed upon women by men anxious to keep women in their place and deny their rights. It was promoted and embraced by women, for it justified education for them, encouraged their political and intellectual interests, commended them for what was in actuality a major part of their lives in the family, and assured them that they

6. Nash, *Women's Education*, 13.
7. Lindley, *You Have Stept*, 5.

could make an important contribution to the public good and America's millennial future."[8]

Dame Schools, Common Schools, and the First Female Seminary

Of course, women were educated to various degrees before the Revolutionary War. At first, in New England education happened in the home. The colonists in America brought with them the belief that the home was a "primary place of education," and the Puritans of Massachusetts quickly passed a law in 1642 stating that children, both male and female, must be taught to read in order to know the scriptures and the local laws that kept society in check.[9] Connecticut issued a similar law in 1650 and New York in 1665. In 1683, Pennsylvania issued an ordinance that parents should teach children "in reading and writing, so that they may be able to read the Scriptures and to write by the time they attain twelve years of age; and that they be taught some useful trade or skill." Servants and orphans were included in these laws as well, with Virginia issuing a law in 1705 requiring that they be made literate and schooled in a trade as well.[10] Girls needed to know how to read and to do basic math in order to read the Bible and to properly run the business of a home.[11] According to the Educational Policy Institute,

> Around the 17th century, basic literacy slowly began to be expected in all classes to ensure religious obedience, and particularly in the New England Colonies, where religious education was paramount, many students attended Dame schools, where working-class families paid a female teacher to provide education out of her home. In 1642, Massachusetts established a law that required all parents guarantee their children capable of reading and understanding "the principles of religion and the capital laws of this country" . . . and five years later, the Old Deluder Satan Act required all towns in Massachusetts with 50 or more families to provide elementary schools and all towns with 100 or more families to establish grammar schools focused on Latin and Greek scholarship.[12]

8. Ibid., 51.

9. Volo and Volo, *Family Life*, 237.

10. Ibid., 238.

11. Educational Policy Institute, "The Landscape of Public Education."

12. Ibid.

In 1635, Boston established the Latin Grammar School, the first secondary school in what would one day be the United States. Also, the public school system in Massachusetts would become the model for the rest of the country by the latter half of the seventeenth century, with religion remaining at the forefront as a concern for educating the young. However, as industry and commerce grew, the emphasis shifted toward using education to produce good citizens more than it was used to produce good Christians. "In 1751, Benjamin Franklin established the Philadelphia Academy" [referenced earlier—this later became the University of Pennsylvania] and in 1783, Noah Webster created the first spelling book designed to promote "democratic ideals."[13] Also, several denominations opened schools, including the Catholics, Quakers, Presbyterians, and Moravians.

For some in America, Dame schools which were prevalent in England were used to educate young children. Dame schools allowed a woman to open her home to local children to teach them basic reading and math and to engage in religious practices.[14] Since girls would not be entering the ministry or a trade, further education was deemed unnecessary. Teachers were untrained and often paid in trade, such as with a cord of wood or a basket of eggs, instead of with money.[15] Often, the Bible was a major textbook and the famous *New England Primer* drew heavily upon it as it sought to iterate the cultural norms, citizenship ideals, and religious precepts prominent at that time.[16] Andrea Wyman, Professor of Elementary Education at Waynesburg College in Pennsylvania, lists several women as the most famous "dames": Hepzibah Pyncheon, "Mrs. Peacock, Good Huswife Jewell, Widow Varnod, Jane Voyer, and Mrs. Jupe."[17] She also lists the most famous of these women, Emma Hart, later known as Emma Hart Willard (1787–1870). She was the founder of Troy Female Seminary, but began by opening a dame school in 1805, and then became preceptress at a female school in Middlebury, Vermont in 1807.[18]

13. Ibid.

14. Eisenmann, *Historical Dictionary*, 90.

15. Wyman, "The Earliest Early Childhood Teachers," 31.

16. Ibid., 30.

17. Ibid., Eisenmann, 32.

18. Martina, "Emma Hart Willard," 1:942.

Adventure Schools

The adventure schools of the mid-eighteenth century were the first schools to teach subjects beyond the basics of reading, writing and math. These schools were run either by a single individual or a married couple who also taught at least one subject, usually a topic that was popular at that time. In addition to the basics, the curriculum included, "music and dancing; drawing and painting; French, Latin, and Greek; fencing, fancy needlework; and just about any other subject for which there might be a market."[19] Adventure schools sprang up all along the East Coast, some single sex for either male or female students and others coed. Unfortunately, the lifespan of these schools tended to be short, as teachers had difficulty making enough money. Adventure schools were "important in themselves, but more important as the predecessors of the more elaborate academy or seminary which, in time, was put upon a firm basis, and in many cases chartered by the states."[20]

Larger communities used "venture schools" that children could attend if their parents paid a fee. Tutors were often employed in the home. In the South, coeducation was common in "dame schools, old field schools, denominational schools, and free schools."[21] Only elite women had a chance for further education, but not in the same subjects as men since men were being prepared for the clergy. Instead, they focused on "music, dance, needlework, art, horseback riding, and French."[22] Finally, the first school for women in America was French and Catholic and can be defined as both a day school and a boarding school. The Ursuline school in New Orleans was opened in 1727 and the nuns taught basic subjects as well as the domestic arts, such as sewing. Few girls were able to secure an education there, but it set an important precedent for women's education outside of the home.

Academies: Ornamental vs. Useful Curriculums

The "next" step in the development of women's education was the female "academy," which tended to have a focus on "ornamental" topics. As Nash has demonstrated, founders of these schools did not use this nomenclature strictly but used "academy," "institute," and "seminary" interchangeably.

19. Nash, *Women's Education*, 36.
20. Woody, *A History of Women's Education*, 1:153.
21. Eisenmann, *Historical Dictionary*, 90.
22. Ibid.

However, for the purposes of this current effort, we will utilize the term "academy" to describe this phase of curriculum development. Whatever the label, of central importance was the fact that women could enroll in academies but could not enroll in "colleges" whose enrollment at that time was restricted to men.

The terms normally associated with the long-standing paradigm regarding women's education in the United States are "ornamental" and "useful." Ornamental refers to education that prepared upper middle class white women in the late eighteenth century to be porcelain wives who were educated in female subjects such as music, art and languages (normally French). "The meaning of the term 'ornamental' remained ambiguous both as to content and as to gender. While some people scornfully regarded 'ornaments' as frivolous, others regarded them as valuable, humanizing influences on men and women alike."[23] Useful education, on the other hand, had the goal of developing women to be critical thinkers and included "male" subjects such as math, science and metaphysics. Study in "useful" subjects was intended to prepare men for professions and, ironically, absent from the framing of male education was any thought of their educational experience making men better husbands and fathers.

The academy movement represented a shift away from home-based education which utilized tutors, to an education provided by teaching professionals in facilities away from home. The academies provided a more formalized education in places of permanence that brought students to locations outside the home where wealthy women could learn with women of other classes. Part of the popularity of academies was that their facilities had the capacity for experiments in science, an academic discipline which was gaining in popularity. This was also a time when the elite class was beginning to embrace the concept that an educational environment away from the home sphere which included competition among students and was a locale for teaching the Republic values—so necessary for the building of a new nation.

Given that the county called "the United States of America" was being developed politically, culturally, and socially, this shift was seen as advancing the development of the Republic. Academies were also seen as the locus for individuals from difference social classes to interact and engage in what today is referred to as "networking"—building relationships beneficial not only on a personal level but also from a career standpoint. Backing belief

23. Nash, *Women's Education*, 42.

with financial backing, many of the academies of the late eighteenth century received state charters thus giving these schools a sense of sustainability.

From a curricular viewpoint, these academies differed from the men's colleges of that era in that the academies offered a more "practical" education. Men's colleges tended to offer a Classical education that focused on Latin and Greek. Critics at the time advocated for a curriculum for men that was centered on the teaching of English rather than "dead languages" and the inclusion of practical courses like "navigation, agriculture and surveying."[24]

The late eighteenth century was a time of ambivalence and debate as to the differentiation between "ornamental" and "useful" education and the value of each to the development of individuals. When it came to courses taught in academies along the continuum of ornamental and useful subjects, there was often disagreement as to which courses were truly ornamental and which were useful and to which gender they should be taught. Depending on the educator, reading, writing, arithmetic, history, geography, and astronomy could fall in one or the other category. Subjects such as dance, music, drawing and reciting were seen both as having value and as a remnant of an aristocratic past that needed to be discarded as the new republic matured.

Ornamental subjects were seen both as unnecessary by some educators and by others as part of a core curriculum to provide a humanizing effect. There also seemed to be ambivalence about women's speech. Women were not expected to speak in public, and in fact women speaking in public, especially to audiences that included both genders, were frowned upon. However, it was believed that women should speak with "proper diction, tone and pronunciation."[25]

In advertising these academies, the greater the variety of academic disciplines offered, the greater the consumer attraction for these schools. Given the tendency to publish a listing of subjects taught as a means of attracting new students, and a dearth of enrollment records from that time era, it is difficult to say which of the courses of study were actually taught in these academies and how many students were enrolled in them. With the advent of the seminaries, their publications would list both subjects taught and the names of students enrolled in the schools.

The founding of the Female Academy at Medford, Massachusetts is seen as the beginning of the Academy movement. This school tenure was

24. Ibid., 38.
25. Ibid., 44.

short lived but made the case for the utility of "female education." In addition to reading, writing, French, dancing, music and embroidery, arithmetic was part of a progression to the study of the earth. The progression to geography was "cyphering" followed by geometry which then qualified students to study geography.[26]

Of all the subjects taught in the academies, there was universal agreement that English studies was of central importance. The range of skills that make up for competency in English include: "reading, writing, spelling orthography, grammar, composition, speaking and oratory or rhetoric."[27] In academies for both genders, reading, writing and spelling were part of the curriculum although the approach to teaching these subjects varied. "Instructors considered spelling and orthography to be different skills, and schools did not necessarily teach them both. Students learned spelling by recitation; the teacher listened as students spelled words out loud. Orthography, however, was a written skill, and schools that emphasized reading over writing did not teach orthography."[28]

The emphasis on writing and orthography in late eighteen century paralleled the development of a growing cash economy and the increased need for written communication. "A cash economy, more than a barter economy, required the ability to read, write and do sums. New types of labor required new types of workers, and the desire to create a national identity required some form of 'Americanizing' of youth. Government 'of the people, by the people, for the people' required a citizenry that was informed and could think clearly."[29]

While men's colleges of the time tended to focus on classical education that focused on Latin and Greek, the curriculum in the academies was more "practical" for the preparation of women who would be the wives of men of means—drawing, painting and music. While these three courses fell most definitely within the category of "ornamental subjects," during this time period which academic disciplines were also "ornamental" was a subject of debate. Reading, writing, geography, astronomy, and arithmetic were also seen to important areas of study as part of "ornamental education."

The traditional paradigm tends to ascribe "ornamental" education to the female academies which came into being first and "useful" education to

26. Woody, *A History of Women's Education*, 1:156.
27. Nash, *Women's Education*, 43.
28. Ibid.
29. Ibid., 2.

the seminaries which was the next permutation in female education. This paradigm also designates that "ornamental" education was for women and "useful" education for men. Nash has demonstrated that the lines of demarcation are not as hard and fast as previously thought, although the intent of education of the genders remained clear: educating men for professions and their roles in the public sphere and educating women for the roles as wives and mothers in the home sphere.

The centerpiece of education reform in the 1800s was providing publicly funded free education to children through what were called common schools. Paralleling this, the country was in an expansionist move both economically and geographically. This meant that job opportunities were expanding for men. Women, then, were in the intersection of the growing need for teachers and the exodus of men from the teaching, a profession that they had up to that time they had dominated.

Seminaries: Educating Teachers and Mothers

Paralleling changes in America's economy and education system was the genesis of the female seminary. These schools had a fourfold purpose: "Christianizing the nation, building a common school system, employing women as teachers and women preparing for self-sufficiency."[30] This next step in the development of women's education also included a shift from rote memorization to learning experiences aimed at developing critical thinking. "The female seminary movement aimed to teach women not what to think but how to think."[31]

The onset of evangelicalism within the landscape of American religious life as a result of the First and Second Great Awakening brought along with it the concept of equal responsibility of men and women before God and an equal responsibility to be "useful" in the kingdom of God. Women played a key role in these revival movements as they tended to be the majority gender in these meetings. Because grace was seen to be bestowed by God equally whether an individual was male or female, "Significantly, it was the experience of grace that gave authority, not formal theological training, thus opening the door for women as well as black men."[32]

---

30. Ibid., 54.

31. Sweet, "Female Seminary," 47.

32. Lindley, *You Have Stept*, 43.

Theologically, postmillennialism of the second Great Awakening dominated the evangelical world. According to this paradigm of the "end times," Christ's return to earth would follow a thousand year time period of optimal conditions in the world. Christians looking around them at the living conditions and social ills that accompanied the growth of cities—poverty, orphans, prostitution—saw that present conditions were a far cry from the glorious kingdom of God promised in the Bible that was to be experienced during the millennium. "Coinciding with an increasing commitment to egalitarian social arrangements, this new pietism led Americans to declare a religious war upon the poverty of their cities. The victory they expected would bring both the conversion of the urban poor and, they believed, of necessity, an end to poverty itself."[33]

While the scope of this book is focused on women's education, it is important to note that during the nineteenth century women were engaged in social reforms including abolitionism and later the suffrage movement. "Women with a broad range of religious backgrounds worked for reforms, but they soon found they faced a double challenge. Like their male counterparts, they had to convince others to join them in a particular cause: but they discovered that they were also forced to defend their right as women to step out of their place to act and organize in a public way."[34]

With the onset of the nineteenth century, educational reforms intersected in a way that was beneficial for women: the development of the common schools and the requisite of teachers for those added classrooms across the country. There was also a growing acceptance of women remaining single and marrying later in life. This was brought about in part by changed in the country's commercial economy and "at a time of increasing numbers of single women and later marriage because of the new capitalist order, some clergy began to defend single women."[35]

The growing need for teachers led to calls for improvements in women's education. The 1820s and 1830s was a "systematic order of subjects"[36] with an intent to provide with a "thorough" education. "The years 1820–1850 were characterized by a remarkable transition in American education. A decisive shift occurred in the philosophy and patterns of educating

33. Smith-Rosenberg, 43.
34. Lindley, *You Have Stept*, 90.
35. Sweet, "Female Seminary," 50.
36. Nash, *Women's Education*, 82.

American women which would have marked social, economic, and political ramifications in antebellum America."[37]

The exemplars that are normally pointed to in the seminary movement are Troy Female Seminary (New York), founded by Emma Willard in 1821, Hartford Female Seminary (Connecticut), founded by Catharine Beecher in 1832, and Mount Holyoke Female Seminary (Massachusetts), founded by Mary Lyon in 1837. These schools were founded in an era of educational reform in which there calls for a more systematic approach to curriculum. The terms "systematic" and "thorough" were terms often used by educators in describe their goal for the revised curriculum. This shift/movement was accompanied by calls for an equal mirroring of curriculum between that offered to men and women.

Willard initially attempted to gain public funding through the New York legislature, but failing that, she turned to the citizens of Troy for funding. According to her vision of female education, intellectually stimulating learning experiences would bring about "a new and happy era in the history of her sex, and of her country and of mankind." While the legislature didn't buy into her dream the wealthy citizens of Troy did and saw the school as an opportunity for their daughters to be educated and Troy Female Seminary was founded. Willard especially promoted math as a part of the curriculum of her school as she saw this curricular emphasis a significant advancement in women education in America.

The seminary provided for the privileged young women a rigorous course of study. "One student reported that she had learned, 'reading, writing, spelling, arithmetic, grammar, geography, history, maps, the globe, algebra, geometry, trigonometry, astronomy, natural philosophy, chemistry, botany, physiology, mineralogy, geography, and zoology,'—and that was just the morning classes!"[38]

The focus of female seminaries on preparing women to be teachers intersected with the discovery by many communities that women could be hired to teach at half the price it cost to hire men. "If then women were properly fitted by instruction, they would be likely to teach children better than the other sex; they could afford to do it cheaper; and those men who would otherwise be engaged in this employment, might be at liberty to add to the wealth of the nation, by any of those thousand occupations, from

---

37. Sweet, "Female Seminary," 41.

38. Cott, *No Small Courage*, 196.

which women are necessarily debarred."[39] Willard was a strong advocate of women entering the field of teaching and by 1850 more than 200 graduates of Troy Seminary had entered the teaching profession.

Going into teaching was beneficial to women because it provided a measure of economic independence before getting married. And if the woman were to become widowed, she would have the training and expertise to open her own school, which would provide a means for her to support financially herself and her children. This latter was a way in which a number of middle and upper class women avoided poverty after the death of their husbands.

Although Willard did not succeed in gaining public funding for Troy Seminary, Mary Lyon was able to take Willard's model and succeed. Lyon was able to gain public and private financing for her Mount Holyoke Female Seminary (later Mount Holyoke College) and eventually it became the first endowed institution of female higher education in America.

In terms of curriculum, while Troy Seminary emphasized a breath of knowledge in its course offerings, Mount Holyoke's focus was on depth of scope in sequence in its curriculum as it became the first female seminary to offer a four-year program of study. Lyon also developed classes in which women discussed current political and social questions thus providing them with an opportunity to develop their own ideas. Science was also an important at Mount Holyoke and every effort was made to keep up with the latest scientific theories and the school provided a small laboratory for students to conduct experiments. "Science classes were frequently taught by Professor Hitchcock, who gave lectures on human anatomy in the 1840s illustrated by the most advanced equipment, including a manikin with detachable organs."[40]

Catharine Beecher believed that women were particularly well suited to become teachers because their moral superiority to men. As far as teaching as a career option for women, "She wanted teaching to become a 'profession for woman, a profession as honorable and as lucrative for her as the legal, medical and theological professions are for men.'"[41] Although she founded Hartford, the main significance of her work was the promotion and advocacy of women's education and her focus on training women as teachers and sending them across the country to start schools in frontier

39. Woody, *A History of Women's Education*, 1:311.
40. Berkin and Norton, *Women of America*, 198.
41. Cott, *No Small Courage*, 265.

communities. About 450 teachers trained by Beecher had founded such schools by the 1850s.

Mary Lyon had identified the need to establish a placement service for women, and in response to this identified need Beecher wrote to Lyon, "my hope is not in women considerably advanced in age, who expect to remain married; it is in young ladies scarcely out of their teens, whose souls are burning for some channel into which they can pour their benevolence, and who will teach two, three, or four years and then marry and become firm pillars to hold up their successors. If we could find teachers, who, unmarried, would devote twenty or thirty years to this work, we would not find as much as by such a circulating system."[42]

While Mount Holyoke also place a crucial role in training teachers, a primary motivation of Mary Lyon in this endeavor was religious. "The work of supplying teachers is a great work, and it must be done, or our country is lost, and the world will remain unconverted."[43] America was still in the afterglow of the religious revival and missionary impetus brought about by the Second Great Awakening and this figured into Lyon's motivation for the founding of her seminary. "It is to be based entirely on Christian principles; and while it is to be furnished with teachers of the highest character and experience, and to have every advantage which the state of female education in this country will allow, its brightest feature will be, that it is a school for Christ."[44]

Also, because missionary organizations would not sponsor single women, a number of Mount Holyoke graduates found fulfillment of their religious calling by serving as the wives of missionaries. These women encountered the phenomenon of "women's work for women," ministering and educating women and children in foreign lands while their husbands did the preaching. The opportunities for teaching went beyond primitive schools in the rural areas of the West and the common schools of the bigger cities as a number of Mount Holyoke went on to become teachers at other female seminaries.

Although emphasis on faith development and commitment to Christian work would diminish by the middle of the nineteenth century, the Christian faith was foundational to student life at female seminaries. "Willard, Lyon, and Beecher were all devout Christians, and they used explicit religious justifications openly in their appeals for support. Moreover,

42. Woody, *A History of Women's Education*, 1:321.

43. Berkin and Norton, *Women of America*, 200.

44 Ibid., 199.

religion was a pervasive influence at their schools, both as part of the regular curriculum and in the periodic revivals they fostered on campus."[45]

Additionally, although women's education in its earliest forms was intended to produce better wives and mothers, it ultimately prepared women for the first societally accepted vocation for women outside the home—teaching. "Female seminaries aimed at providing women with a broad liberal cultural outlook which transcended the domestic frame of mind. The movement was based on a paradox that only an education that did not prepare women specifically to be wives and mothers could prepare women adequately to be wives and mothers."[46]

With the onset of normal schools, educational institutions founded primary to prepare women teachers, in the mid-1800s, and women's colleges, enrollments grew exponentially. In 1870 almost 11,000 women were attending seminaries of colleges and by 1900 that number had jumped to 85,000.[47] Women demonstrated and continue to demonstrate that their mental acumen was equal to that of men and the whether the curriculum was ornamental, practical or useful, women not only were capable of engaging it, but would also achieve mastery in whatever subject they studied.

Parallel Streams—African American and Native American Seminaries

While there are separate chapters in this book on African American and Native American female seminaries in which the curriculum of these schools is discussed, it is important to note motivations that are important for the framing of those educational experiences. Among African Americans, the development of female seminaries was yet another milestone in the efforts of self-improvement and community-based educational efforts by African Americans. This educational endeavor also dovetailed well with concerns of white Americans in the aftermath of the Emancipation. They saw educational opportunities for African Americans as a way to create a genteel "talented tenth" of the African Americans—a version of "house Negro"—who would serve as a buffer should the "field Negroes" rise up in revolt and want to exact their revenge for the ravages that slavery caused their people. Female seminaries among Native Americans education were

45. Lindley, *You Have Stept*, 92.
46. Sweet, "Female Seminary," 49.
47. Nash, *Women's Education*, 115.

part of a strategy developed by whites to Christianize Native Americans and annihilate their indigenous tribal culture with an end goal of achieving in Native American students assimilation into white culture. To conclude, it is important to note the education has been one of the most influential and enduring tools of social control, for good or for ill, since the colonists first arrived. Thus, curriculum is representative of the very tools that have shaped Americans over the centuries and encapsulates our strengths and our shortcomings as a society over time.

6

The Self-Sustaining Impulse
and the Talented Tenth:
African American Seminaries

African American Female Seminaries

Charlottesville, VA., Oct. 17, 1866

Mrs. Gibbins (a colored native teacher) is very much liked by the colored people here. Her nature is so noble, that she is not so liable to stimulate petty jealousy among her people as many might under similar circumstances . . . I think she is doing well in her new sphere of duty, especially in the matter of government. She has a kind of magnetism about her which is a good qualification for a teacher. She is really a fine reader of easy readings, and I should choose her to prepare scholars for me in that line, from among nine-tenths of those engaged in this work, so far as I have known her. She intends to pursue her studies in the evening with my help.

Anna Gardner, *The Freedmen's Record*, Vol. 2, No. 11[1]

So, WHERE DOES THE journey start for African American women to this place of educational empowerment? The journey begins in the tribal lands of Africa which were invaded by slave traders and as a result, African women and men were loaded onto ships in preparation to cross the Middle

---

1. Lerner, *Black Women in White America*, 103.

Passage. Once on the ships, while the African men were in chains below deck with barely enough breathing room, the women were able to stay on the quarterdeck without the restraint of chains. This made them available and susceptible to the sexual assault of the crew staffing the slave ship.

Upon arrival in America, these African women and their male counterparts were put up for sale to be utilized for slave labor. The women of highest value were those of child bearing age who bodies looked like they could bear multiple children with few health risks. Once purchased, these women either worked in the field or were bought in order to be sexual partners or wives for male slaves. In addition to field work, these women also served as domestics in the plantation house, nurses, midwives and at times, de facto mothers of the plantation owners' children. And, just because a slave woman was "married" to a fellow slave did not mean that she escaped having to engage in sexual encounters with an overseer or the slave master. As mothers, these women at times watched helpless as their offspring were sold to work in a distant plantation when their children became of age for such a financial transaction.

Given these very oppressive beginnings, what does the journey look like from the plantation to the founding of the Atlanta Baptist Female Seminary, the school that would become Spelman College, America's oldest historically black college for women? The trajectory of education for African American women in the United States is very much opposite from that of white women. Indeed, following the Middle Passage journey from Africa to America, slave masters were intentional about prohibiting African American women and men from becoming literate let alone highly educated. While the journey was been difficult and full of difficulties, African American women would benefit from the struggle of their white sisters to obtain equitable access to educational opportunities afforded to white men.

"The history of the education of Negro women, therefore, does not parallel exactly the history of education of white women. While Oberlin College opened in 1833 for the admission of all races and both sexes, there was a long period of struggle for the admission of women to college, but, by the time of the founding of Vassar College in 1865, at least three Negro women had been awarded the degree of Bachelor of Arts. By the time any considerable number of Negro women were ready for college, the question of the right of women to a college education had been, to all intents and purposes, settled."[2]

2. Slowe, "Higher Education of Negro Women," 352.

While much has been written about the two-sphere "home" and "public" paradigm in regards to white women in America, this paradigm was not applicable to African American women, especially during the antebellum era. For African Americans, the "public sphere" of the workplace would be shared equally by men and women, and the separate "public sphere" of oratory would not occur until the Christianization of African American slaves, especially in the first half of the nineteenth century. Although in most circumstances speaking under the authority and careful ear of a white counterpart, African Americans began to fill the role of preacher, although for the most part, this religious role came to be the domain of males.

African American women, as was and continues to be the case with women of all ethnicities, were essential in the development of the church. Numerically their gender was the majority in congregations and women had key worship roles within the early Christian gatherings of slaves. It is thought that because of the experience of slavery, African American women especially, found a special place for Jesus in their hearts. "More than any others, black women historically have embraced Jesus Christ. Enslaved women discovered a Jesus who seemed to speak directly to them and to their painful and protracted struggle for freedom. They saw in their condition a parallel to the suffering and persecution that Jesus had endured—Jesus was crucified, and many enslaved Africans were beaten, maimed, and killed."[3]

Within the context of plantation life, African American woman were not seen through eyes that assessed her intellectual or scholastic acumen but rather through eyes that keep her captive within one of two predominant myths[4]—"Jezebel," a promiscuous woman, or as "Mammy," the ideal of domestic help within the big house of the plantation. "In antebellum America, the female slave's chattel status, sex and race combined to create a complicated set of myths about black womanhood."[5]

As a "Jezebel," African American women were viewed as a counterpart to the Victorian ideals of virtue and piety and were instead seen as being controlled by their sensuality and thus readily available to the slave master. In part, this myth arose from European slave traders' perceptions of cultural factors including African women's attire in their native land, the practice of polygamy and tribal dances.

3. Collier-Thomas, *Jesus, Jobs, and Justice*, 10.

4. White, *Ar'n't I a Woman*, 27–61.

5. Ibid., 28.

The "Mammy," on the other hand, was a superwoman of domesticity, who could run the master's house with extraordinary mastery and at the same time was known for her love for the white children of the master. Her level of respect within the "Big House" was such that at times she served as advisor to both her master and her mistress. In either case, these women were powerless regarding the fate of their children and of themselves. In reality, when they were no longer useful, they were discarded by the plantation owners.

Opposition to Education

Although separated by a little over a century, two events would negatively impact Southerners' attitudes toward African American literacy: the Stono Slave Rebellion and the Nat Turner Revolt. In the Stono Rebellion of 1739, over twenty whites were killed by slaves attempting to escape to Florida. In 1842, the revolt led by Nat Turner in Southampton County, Virginia, cost the lives of 55 to 65 whites, and over 100 slaves killed in the aftermath of the rebellion. Each event led to restrictions, both in terms of anti-literacy laws and punishments for slaves who tried to learn to read and write.

The most severe of these punishments were whippings and amputations. The objections to slave literacy was threefold: 1) the slaves did not have the mental acumen for formal education and would only become confused; 2) slaves might learn to forge passes to non-slave states; and, 3) insurrection and rebellion might result from slaves reading abolitionist writings. "More important ideologically, keeping the masses of African Americans illiterate contributed to the myth of racial inferiority, a conveniently circular logic: blacks were intellectually incapable of mastering the skills of literacy; illiterate blacks were proof of black intellectual incapacity."[6]

Evangelicalism and Education

However, nothing could stop African American slaves from satisfying their hunger for knowledge. Within the antebellum environs the main source book for literacy was the Bible. "The testimony of ex-slaves repeatedly noted how significant it was to read the Bible, write one's name, compute

---

6. Butchart, *Schooling the Freed*, 2.

one's earnings, and teach others to do the same."[7] Religious plantation owners were caught in a dichotomy of wanting to keep slaves illiterate and at the same share the Gospel of salvation and the moral teachings in Scripture. From a utilitarian perspective, the Bible was a great source for teaching slaves their "divine" roles as slaves and the subservience that they were to show their masters. Even though plantation owners wanted to keep their slaves illiterate, there was also an important need for some level of literacy among a select few of the slaves to carry out tasks on the plantation like record keeping.

When allowed the opportunity for Christian teaching, slaves were very familiar with the truncated singular message they would hear in church. According to Beverly Jones, a former slave in Virginia, "Niggers had to set an' listen to the white man's sermon, but they didn't want to 'cause they knowed it by heart. Always took his text from Ephesians, the white preacher did, the part what said, 'Obey your masters, be [a] good servant' . . . They always tell the slaves dat ef he be good, an' worked hard fo' his master, dat he would go to heaven, an' der he gonna live a life of ease. They ain' never tell he gonna be free in Heaven. You see, they didn' want slaves to start thinkin' 'bout freedom, even in Heaven."[8]

The Second Great Awakening (1790–1840) put at the forefront the belief that all men and women from every race was equally responsible to God and therefore in need of salvation through belief in Jesus Christ. A parallel core tenet was the need for all redeemed individuals to be "useful" for the kingdom of God. Since all were in need of salvation that meant that within the South, the Gospel must be preached to slaves and slave masters alike. The efforts to reach the African American in the bondage of slavery for Jesus resulted in the "planation missions" movement of the 1830s and 1840s. The long-term impact was that African Americans who embraced this faith tradition not only became members of congregations but also its advocates as preachers, ministers and founders of churches and denominations.

During this time in the South, there were a number of Baptist and Methodist churches and there were opportunities for a select few slaves to hear the Gospel when they attended church with their masters. Yet, the vast majority of slaves on the planation were beyond the scope of this

---

7. Higginbotham, *Righteous Discontent*, 19.

8. Collier-Thomas, *Jesus, Jobs, and Justice*, 6.

opportunity. Spreading out from South Carolina and Georgia, plantation missions were established throughout the South.

For the plantation owners and for white Southerners, there were a number of issues to be dealt with regarding this egalitarian evangelical movement. Since there was fierce opposition to literacy among slaves, what form would religious instruction take following religious conversion? Would becoming a Christian lead a slave to docility or rebellion since the Bible and evangelical teaching could be utilized to foster either outcome? For Southerners, this was especially important because abolitionism, the movement to end slavery, was gaining momentum. Ironically, the more radical abolitionists were provided with religious justifications for ending slavery as a result of the Second Great Awakening on their lives and beliefs.

"The abolitionist movement created ambivalence in Southern thought about the instruction of slaves. On the one hand, the fear that abolitionist literature would incite slave rebellion tended to have a chilling effect on any kind of instruction for slaves. On the other hand, abolitionist arguments against slavery challenged proslavery apologists to push slave evangelization as one of the strongest proofs that slavery was a positive good."[9]

Plantation missions were part of a greater reform movement to bring about holiness across the nation and if it was to be truly national in scope it had to include the Negro slave. To accomplish this, leaders of this movement had to demonstrate to the plantation owners and the white Southern power structure that its religious efforts was not antithetical to slavery. Given the geo-centricity of the South, there would also be resistance by the planters if plantation missions reported to national boards so the efforts and associations that coordinated these proselytizing efforts had to be local in scope and control. Additionally, there was resistance from Southerners because they believed that African Americans didn't have the capacity for religious experience. "Some masters did not allow their slaves to go to church and ridiculed the notion of religion for slaves because they refused to believe that Negroes had souls. Others forbade their slaves to attend church because, as an ex-slave explained, 'White folks 'fraid the niggers git to thinkin' they are free, if they had church and things.'"[10]

Ultimately, the efforts of plantation missions were fruitful and quite a number of slaves were won over to Christianity. Once converted, how would religious instruction be carried out? What follows was an interplay

9. Raboteau, *Slave Religion*, 158.

10. Ibid., 220.

between Northern and Southern churches with the churches of the North calling their Southern counterparts to account regarding the need to appropriately instruct slaves in their newly found faith commitment. What resulted was a sixfold process of religious instruction: 1) regular sermons geared toward the perceived level of the slaves' mental capacity; 2) a weekly lecture which the master and his family were encouraged to attend in order to provide a good example for his slaves; 3) Sabbaths schools for all ages; 4) the instruction in these school was limited to oral delivery, "religion without letters" utilizing a question and answer method from printed catechisms, homilies and visual aids to achieve learning; and, 5) regular gatherings which included only slave converts; and 6) that the plantation owner would approve and know where these meetings were held.[11]

As a result of the Emancipation Proclamation and the successful conclusion of the Civil War, African Americans and the greater United States were presented with opportunities and challenges in attempting to achieve a high level of education for African Americans, but for all of the country's citizens.

In the postbellum South, a number of initiatives were carried out to educate freed slaves whose literacy rate was 5 percent in 1860.[12] The foundation for these efforts came from the freed slave themselves. "Former slaves were the first among native southerners to depart from the planters' ideology of education and society and campaign for universal, state-sponsored public education. In their movement for universal schooling the ex-slaves welcomed and actively pursued the aid of Republican politicians, the Freedman's Bureau, northern missionary societies, and the Union Army."[13]

As African Americans emerged from slavery into freedom, the church became central to their communal life and a foundation for many of the self-improvement initiatives in the area of education. "More effectively than any other institution, the church stood between individual blacks, on the one hand, and the state with its racially alienating institutions, on the other. The church's ability to sustain numerous newspapers, schools, social welfare services, jobs, and recreational facilities mitigated the dominant society's denial of these resources to the black communities."[14] Two denominations that dominated this key role are the African Methodist Episcopal

11. Ibid., 162.

12. Higginbotham, *Righteous Discontent*, 11.

13. Anderson, *The Education of Blacks*, 4.

14. Higginbotham, *Righteous Dicontent*, 9.

and the Black Baptist Church. Both were breakaway institutions from their white mother denominations.

As Northern missionary societies and the U.S. Bureau of Refugees, Freeman and Abandoned Lands (Freedmen's Board) entered the South in the postbellum era to educate African Americans, they found that instead of bringing education to African Americans, they would be building on educational efforts already established by slaves and freed persons of color. These included a school founded in 1861 in Fort Monroe, Virginia by Mary Peake, a black teacher, and a school operating in Savannah, Georgia from 1833 to 1865 whose teacher was a woman named Deveaux.[15]

White teachers, mainly from the Northeast, joined a cadre of African Americans, who through their efforts of self-improvement, had achieved some level of education. "After slavery many of the leading black educators emerged from among the rebel literates, those slaves who had sustained their own learning process in defiance of the slave owners' authority. They viewed literacy and formal education as means to liberation and freedom."[16]

Across the South, newly freed African Americans gave of their meager resources toward the fulfillment of the dream that they and especially their children would gain the education that for them symbolized equality of personhood and equality of citizenship. "Out of their great poverty they raised funds to buy land for their schools, supplied the labor to build the schools, supported teachers as best as they could, and maintained such an effective network of schools across the South after the Civil War that W. E. B. DuBois could argue that the postwar system of southern public education arose from the foundation laid by the freed people."[17] Not only did African American improve their own educational environment and opportunities, but they also helped improve education for whites by challenging the planters' (plantation owners) educational paradigm that schooling happened in the home and not in public schools.

One of the important developments in the immediate postbellum era was the academy. Modeled on their New England predecessors, these educational institutions played a significant role in the education of African Americans. Founded as early as 1865 these schools would continue to operate in the South as late at 1935. Most academies were church-related and established by a number of denominations: African Methodist Episcopal,

15. Anderson, *The Education of Blacks*, 7.

16. Ibid., 17.

17. Butchart, *Schooling of the Freed People*, 1–2.

Presbyterian, Lutheran, Congregational, and Quaker. "These school ranged from primary schools to high schools to normal schools for the training of teachers who would go on to teach in other black schools."[18]

The academies were primarily parochial day or boarding schools and the curricular focus was on reading, writing and mathematics although courses in cooking, sewing, and domestic arts were also offered. The study of the Bible was required, and music, especially singing, was central part of learning experience for students in these schools. When these schools were first started the hope of students was that they would gain basic literacy so they could read the Bible, complete basic math computations, and understand labor contracts.

Because of the travel distance between home and school, a number of these academies became boarding schools. Students in the boarding schools received round the clock attention from the adults who were charged with helping shape their moral character and social graces. The intended end result of this educational model was that "boarding students would gain strength, poise and personal pride; appreciation for the property of others, and a knowledge of how to live independently."[19]

A classical liberal arts curriculum dominated the boarding schools, at first taught by white teachers who gained their expertise in New England academies and then taught by African American teachers as they took over instruction. Practical courses in industrial arts were added to the curriculum, although the emphasis was on Latin, algebra, English literature, and foreign languages such as Greek, French, and German. The Avery Normal Institute, founded by the American Missionary Association (AMA) in Charleston, South Carolina, had such a curriculum.

Charlotte Hawkins Brown, a self-proclaimed disciple of Booker T. Washington, founded Palmer Memorial Institute, had a different perspective than her role model and steadfastly resisted efforts to make industrial education an emphasis at her school. Instead, she utilized a college preparatory approach in which her students studied Latin, French, English, algebra, geometry, and science. To balance out the students' educational experience, students took courses in agriculture, home economics and industrial education, and helped raise food for the school by working on a 120-acre farm. Brown's school was representative of the tension experienced by my

18. Durham, "The Other Side of the Story," 4.
19. Ibid., 5.

academies in choosing which curriculum to offer and/or to emphasize: classical education or industrial education.

As has been stated a number of denominations participated in founding academies for African Americans throughout the South. The flow of money and white teachers from the North were very instrumental in establishing these schools. Equally important is the fact that African Americans themselves participated in the founding of these schools initially by helping raise the monies to support their funding and later by providing the cadre of African American teachers would teach in these schools. The schools demonstrated that, contrary to the belief of many Southern whites, African Americans valued education and saw it as the "pearl of great price." However, that these schools did not produce a level of property ownership and economic self-sufficiency among its graduates can be explained in the context of racist structures of society at that time.

That said, "The great contribution of African-American academies is that they took students from both rural and urban settings and nurtured them in a caring environment which modeled character and also provided a high quality education. The best testimonial to the quality of education received is provided by the hundreds of graduates who went on to college and became useful citizens, contributing to their professions and the larger society."[20]

The Talented Tenth and Founding of the Atlanta Baptist Female Seminary

In 1896, Henry Morehouse coined the term "Talented Tenth" to make the case that developing an African American elite was essential for the advancement of all blacks. "I repeat that not to make proper provision for the high education of the talented tenth man of the colored colleges is a prodigious mistake. It is to dwarf the tree that has in it the promise of a grand oak. Industrial education is good for the nine; the common English branches are good for the nine; the tenth man ought to have the best opportunities for making the most of himself for humanity and God."[21]

This concept had appeal for both African Americans and Northern missionary groups, especially the American Baptist Home Missions Society (ABHMS). For the ABHMS, it was essential that higher education for

20. Ibid., 13.

21. Higgenbotham, *Righteous Discontent*, 25.

women was given equal value as the educational for men, that is was as essential to develop the "Female Talented Tenth" as it was its male counterpart. The organization viewed educational policies that excluded women as counterproductive to the overall success of African American. Although not totally altruistic in their beliefs, "These motives, both egalitarian and self-serving, came to be articulated through the concept of the Talented Tenth. Indeed the very concept came to life with the rise of black Baptist colleges and represented the philosophical basis upon which the missionary educators sought to transform black America."[22]

Three overarching goals were being accomplished through the development of the female talented tenth: 1) a leadership cadre of teachers and administrators would lead efforts to educate the poor masses and illiterate African Americans; 2) by example, these members of the Talented Tenth would inculcate white middle class values and behaviors including refined manners; and, 3) a "buffer" class would be created that would stand between whites and the masses of African Americans.

Some of the proponents of the female Talented Tenth saw great promise for African American women in this effort to produce this elite cadre. Thomas Jefferson Morgan believed that women's education should be equally crafted and challenging as that of men and that African American women had equal intellectual and cultural capabilities as black men and white women. While Morgan believed that higher education was beneficial for the domestic life of African American women, the greater value was in preparing these women for professional careers. "Higher education also equipped Black women to earn a living—an especially important function since, as Morgan noted, economic necessity forced large numbers of them to work. Venturing an optimistic prediction of widening employment opportunities, he contended that college training would prepare black women to keep pace with changes in coming decades."[23]

Although it was established seventeen years before the term was coined, the Atlanta Baptist Female Seminary would come to exemplify the best of strategies by the ABHMS in establishing the Female Talented Tenth. The success of the school and its alumni came to justify all the ABHMS' investment both in terms of human resources and money, in this school and other that were founded and funded by this missionary organization.

22. Ibid.
23. Ibid., 29.

The foundation of the female seminary that would become Spelman College was a crossroads of self-improvement efforts of African American in the South and the aspirations of Sophia B. Packard and Harriet E. Giles, two white women who were teachers and Baptist missionaries from New England, to one day open their own school. Packard and Giles met at the New Salem Academy in Massachusetts where Packard was a teacher and preceptress and Giles was a student. Even though there was an eleven-year difference in age between the two women, they became good friends and engaged in religious activities together. After leaving the New Salem Academy, the two women taught at a village school in Petersham, the Connecticut Literary Institution, and The Oread Collegiate Institute.

As part of her involvement in Christian leadership, Packard was the chair of the meeting of the Women's American Baptist Home Missionary Society (WABHMS) when it was formed in Boston in 1877. In 1880, Packard and Giles journeyed to the South and visited institutions that served African Americans including Fisk University, elementary schools and churches and the two women returned to Boston with "filled with a desire to start a school." Speaking of the conviction that gripped their hearts, Giles recounted in retrospect in 1896 how "their eyes were opened [by the Southern trip] to the appalling need to help for the colored women and girls. The conviction was profoundly impressed on them that their lives should be given to the education and Christianization of these downtrodden people."[24]

Giles and Packard had to raise their own financial support (Giles even sold her piano, a significant personal sacrifice), in order to help raise funds. Ironically, the two women also had to overcome opposition from the WABHMS to their journey to the South. Spiritually, they needed to be assured that the project they were undertaking was part of God's divine plan. "Dear Master, do Thou lead me to know fully what Thy will to me is and what Thou would have me to do and where to labor,"[25] Packard wrote in her diary in January, 1881.

Upon arriving in Atlanta on April 1, 1881, they were directed to seek out Rev. Frank Quarles, pastor of Atlanta's Friendship Baptist Church and the most influential African American preacher in Georgia. When Packard and Giles presented their plan for a school, Pastor Quarles said their project was an answer to their prayers as he was very concerned about the

24. Read, *The Story of Spelman College*, 38.
25. Ibid., 37.

lack of educational opportunities for African American women. Quarles called for a meeting of local pastors to gain their support and subsequently, the Atlanta Baptist Female Seminary was founded on April 11, 1881 in the basement of Friendship Baptist Church.

The student body in that first year started with of eleven women, a few who were former slaves and one young girl. Instructional resources in such a rudimentary setting were scarce. "Lacking blackboards, students added and subtracted on the floor. Three recitation classes were heard at once in opposite corners of the basement, while a fourth enjoyed greater privacy in the coal bin."[26] By the end of that first year, enrollment grew to eighty. That basement space soon proved to be inadequate for the rapidly growing number of students.

Fortunately, Packard and Giles were able to tap into the philanthropy of John D. Rockefeller, whom they met with at a church conference in Cleveland, Ohio. With the funds he provided, the two women were able to purchase a nine-acre site once used as an army barracks during the Civil War. In an act of gratitude for the generosity shown by Rockefeller, in 1884, the name of the school was changed to Spelman Seminary in honor of the parents of his wife, Laura Spelman Rockefeller. By 1885, the school had an enrollment of 645 students, 250 of whom were boarding students.

In 1888, Spelman was legally organized with a charter and board of trustees and Packard was appointed president of the school. In 1894 college preparatory classes including Latin were added to the school's curriculum. Industrial education was also an integral part of the instruction. "Founders Sophia Packard and Harriet Giles believed that the legacy of slavery left blacks indolent and in need of proper work habits, and they insisted that an academic education without an internalization of the Protestant work ethic proved more harmful than beneficial."[27] This "domestic education" included dressmaking, housekeeping, laundry work, and cooking. In 1885 when the Slater Fund gifted Spelman a printing press, students were instructed in printing, and like many Black institution, the school produced a newspaper, the Spelman Messenger.

Religion was central to life and learning at Spelman. Packard and Giles considered the religious component so important that they dismissed the benefits of higher education if devoid of missionary spirit."[28] Adopting

26. Higgenbotham, *Righteous Discontent*, 32.

27. Ibid., 33.

28. Ibid., 34.

a school motto of "Our whole school for Christ," the learning paradigm was that religion must both inform and guide secular training, both industrial and college preparatory. Daily devotionals and a systematic study of the Bible was a regular part of student life, and Sundays were fully scheduled with Christian activities: chapel devotion at 8:30 am; at 11:00 am students had a choice between reading the Bible silently or attending a religious service; Sunday School in the afternoon followed by a preaching service. It is no wonder then that the school was imbued with religious fervor as well as it reported more conversions to Christ than any other Baptist school.

In the area of academics the focus was on teacher preparation with the distinction that students were prepared for the "dual capacity as teacher and missionary." In the first years of the school a "normal" department was develop and students learned the basics of teaching. A Model School was established at Spelman in which elementary students were taught by faculty-supervised student teachers. Harriet Giles was instrumental in introducing students at Spelman to the best practices in teaching during that time period. This effort to train students in the most current teaching practices was enhanced by the work of Elizabeth V. Griffin, a Potsdam Normal School graduate, who in 1893 reorganized the normal practice school.

During summers Spelman students in the advanced normal classes would teach throughout rural Georgia and in various locales throughout the south. The class size averaged forty students per classroom and it was estimated that a minimum of 6,000 children were taught by the 150 to 200 Spelman women who dedicated their summers to teaching. One student, Carrie Wells, received special recognition for the quality of instruction in her classroom. "The recitations, the singing, the speaking, reading, spelling, arithmetic and all else were well nigh perfect," noted James Clark, a wealthy white "friend of the race."[29]

Whether African American women graduated from a female seminary like Spelman or one of the other black institutions of higher education, these women saw themselves as "spiritual and intellectual beacons" to their people. At the same time, not all their efforts were received well back home. When the educated, mission-minded women returned to their rural homes, some of their families and members of the communities were resistant to efforts to stop age-old habits of smoking, drinking, and gambling. Given the working class mindset predominant in rural areas, not everyone appreciated the

29. Ibid., 37.

value of education. Other saw the sophistication of college educated women as a concession to assimilation and adoption of white culture.

On the one hand it is the oldest historically black colleges for women in the United States. Like some of its white counterparts, rather than appear on the academic scene as a female seminary and then close some years later, Spelman developed the administration, facilities infrastructure and curriculum to become a college that continues to challenge women to their positions of leadership in society. Like other institution of higher education sponsored by the American Baptist Home Mission Society (ABHMS), Spelman played a key role in developing the Female Talented Tenth so central to the vision of the ABHMS in creating a better place for African Americans in America.

7

The Politics of Assimilation:
The Cherokee Female Seminary

Early Attempts at Education

WHILE MOST PEOPLE IMAGINE that educating Native Americans did not become important until the nineteenth century, historian Cary Michael Carney lists several schools for Native Americans on a timeline, beginning with a school opened in 1536 in Mexico City, or Taltelolco, by Spanish colonists. Although these Native Americans are not the ones we usually think of, these Native Americans to our south attended the academy and alumni ran it between 1536 and 1568.[1] In what is now the United States, next came a college established in Florida by Jesuits for Indians in 1568, then Henrico College in Virginia, which was opened in 1617 thanks to Pocahontas's ability to raise funds from King James I. Next came Harvard's attempt to bring in Native American students beginning in 1645 and close behind was the Indian College in 1656. Following that was William and Mary College's attempt to enroll Native Americans between 1705 and 1721 with the building of Brafferton in 1723 to house them and the arrival of the first student to live there in 1743, and the 1756 founding of Dartmouth for the purpose of educating Native Americans.[2] Though not very successful, by 1776 all ef-

1. Carney, *Native American Higher Education*, 155.
2. Ibid., 155–56.

forts on behalf of educating Native Americans were pushed aside as a result of focus on the Revolutionary War.[3]

Even from the earliest beginnings, the purpose of educating Native Americans involved using both culture and religion to eradicate their cultures. Carney points out on his timeline of important Native American events that discussions about using education to civilize Indians began as far back as 1550 when Bartolome de Las Casas, a Dominican friar, argued that they should not enslave the Indians by following Aristotle's "doctrine of natural slavery," but should use "religion and education as the means to civilize them."[4] Likewise, in Amanda J. Cobb's book, *Listening to Our Grandmother's Stories: The Bloomfield Academy for Chickasaw Females, 1852–1949*, although writing about education centuries later, she reveals the irony of education when it is used for assimilation. Drawing upon a quote from Richard Shaull, the man who wrote the foreword to Paulo Friere's *Pedagogy of the Oppressed*, she illustrates a key point about the irony of Chickasaw education:

> There is no such thing as a *neutral* education process. Education either functions as an instrument that is used to facilitate the integration of the younger generation in the logic of the present system and bring about conformity to it, or it becomes "the practice of freedom," the means by which men and women deal critically and creatively with reality and discover how to participate in the transformation of their world.[5]

In her telling of how girls and young women came to be educated at the Bloomfield (later Carter) Academy, Cobb writes that education became a way to "conquer," not to "discover how to participate in the transformation of their world," as Shaull says.[6] For the Chickasaws, despite the fact that they were complying with whites to "speak English, to become Christian, to educate their children, and to farm" (farming was a way to reject communal living—an anti-capitalist social construction), they were still not white.[7] Cobb quotes Lawrence Cremin: "the prevailing assumption was clear: people could be educated to transcend the barriers of ethnicity and

---

3. Ibid., 157.
4. Ibid., 155.
5. Cobb, *Listening to Our Grandmother's Stories*, 20.
6. Ibid., 5.
7. Ibid., 31–32.

religion in order to become full-fledged members of the American community, but they could not be educated to transcend the barriers of race."[8]

In the United States, religion was combined with education to facilitate assimilation. Congress created the ABCFM, or the American Board of Commissioners for Foreign Missions, in 1810.[9] Founded in Massachusetts, it was to "support American Protestant missionary activities."[10] At first women could only be a part of these activities as wives, but by 1880, they made up 57 percent of missionaries.[11] The ABCFM sent missionaries to the Cherokees in Tennessee in 1817 and to the Choctaws in Mississippi in 1818.[12] In 1819, Congress passed the Indian Civilization Fund Act and offered these missionaries money to educate American Indians.[13] In 1824, they created the Bureau of Indian Affairs (BIA) to administer the funds. An excerpt from the statute is illustrative for why they wished to educate Native Americans and to what extent:

> For the purpose of providing against the further decline and final extinction of the Indian tribes, adjoining the frontier settlements of the United States, and for introducing among them the habits and arts of civilization, the President of the United States shall be, and he is hereby authorized, in every case where he shall judge improvement in the habits and condition of such Indians practicable, and that the means of instruction can be introduced with their own consent, to employ capable persons of good moral character, to instruct them in the mode of agriculture suited to their situation; and for teaching their children in reading, writing and arithmetic.[14]

The BIA used missionary groups to teach Christian doctrine and the "spheres" of men and women, but the missionaries could not make the children attend and sometimes parents would keep them home because of

8. Ibid., 32.

9. Ibid., 22.

10. Eisenmann, *Historical Dictionary*, 47.

11. Ibid., 48. The Women's Board of Missions was formed in 1868 in Boston. They published a journal called *Life and Light for Heathen Women* to inspire women to enter the missions field and to offer advice on teaching (ibid., 49–50).

12. Ibid., 48.

13. Carney, *Native American Higher Education*, 158. Carney notes that funds were also provided to train Native Americans in agriculture. This was considered an appropriate education for them.

14. "The Missionary Impulse."

the difference in beliefs.[15] In 1819, the Presbyterian, Methodist, and Baptist missionary foundations sent their people into the unsettled West. Cobb regards this as the beginning of "colonial education" for Native American children, although her tribe already had one Presbyterian missionary from 1799–1803 who had spent time teaching the children to read and write during his stay.[16] She points out that the partnership between church and state emphasized the hegemonic belief that "Christianity, civilization, and American citizenship were inextricably intertwined."[17]

According to historians Faulk and Welge, the first school opened in Indian Territory was opened by Union Mission, a Presbyterian mission started by the Reverends Chapman and Vaill.[18] It opened on August 27, 1821 and had four Osage children as students.[19] In the 1820s many Presbyterian, Methodist, Baptist, and nondenominational schools opened throughout the Cherokee Nation and although financial and political difficulties resulted in many closing, they converted over one thousand to Christianity.[20] Devon Mihesuah, author of *Cultivating the Rosebuds: The Education of Women at the Cherokee Female Seminary, 1851–1909*, describes a time when the Brainerd Mission in Chattanooga, Tennessee was used to both educate and convert students. Although it was established in 1816, by 1821 it was failing.[21] Mihesuah speculates it could have been because the Cherokee syllabary was developed by Sequoyah in 1821 and the Cherokees might have questioned the need to know another language. She notes that some feared the missionaries would take their lands for payment and the frustration with the missionaries' lack of respect for Cherokee culture.[22]

The American Board and the United Foreign Missionary Society joined forces in 1826 and worked with the tribes in Indian Territory. They had these goals: "conversion of everyone to Christianity, schooling for the children, and vocational education for the adults, along with medical assistance for the sick."[23] In the 1830s and 40s, more schools opened, but in

---

15. Eisenmann, *Historical Dictionary*, 61.

16. Cobb, *Listening to Our Grandmother's Stories*, 26.

17. Ibid., 26–27.

18. Faulk and Welge, *Oklahoma*, 78.

19. Ibid., 78.

20. Mihesuah, *Cultivating the Rosebuds*, 16.

21. Ibid., 8.

22. Ibid., 8.

23. Faulk and Welge, *Oklahoma*, 79.

1838 the Cherokee Nation designed its own public school system.[24] Even after they opened their own school system, the 1827 Cherokee Constitution illustrates that a non-Christian could not hold office in the civil department and that "religion, morality, and knowledge, being necessary to good government, the preservation of liberty and the happiness of mankind, schools, and the means of education shall forever be encouraged in this Nation."[25] Thus, Christianity became ingrained in the culture of those it was once used by outsiders as a tool of control and of assimilation.

In the 1880s, the Bureau of Indian Affairs created off-reservation boarding schools to indoctrinate children more effectively, and children were even taken from parents without their permission, forced to attend. Native Americans feared these schools for several reasons: disease rampant in the schools, total separation from their children sometimes lasting several years and sometimes for forever as some children disappeared, and missing significant tribal initiations which meant they could never be full members of the tribe.[26] Although they had established schools decades before this, the Cherokee tribe was one of the most significant tribes to recognize they needed to take the education of their people into their own hands, but it was not to retain their culture. It was to facilitate assimilation, as can be seen from exploring the history of the Cherokee Female Seminary.

The Cherokee Female Seminary

Before they could open a female seminary in what would one day be the state of Oklahoma, the Cherokees had to be moved there. They did not go quietly. Despite the stereotypes created and reinforced by fiction and film, Native Americans were able to shrewdly navigate a culture, a language, and a legal system foreign to them at one time. Prior to their removal, the Cherokees had devised a republican form of government in the 1820s and instituted a police force for each of its eight districts.[27] The constitution they adopted in 1827 was modeled, in part, on the Constitution of the United States and created a government with legislative, judicial, and executive branches. They held elections to elect their Chief and they controlled annuities, but the Georgians ignored all of this once gold was discovered in

24. Mihesuah, *Cultivating the Rosebuds*, 16–17.

25. Ibid., 18.

26. Eisenmann, *Historical Dictionary*, 62.

27. Mihesuah, *Cultivating the Rosebuds*, 12.

1828 in Dahlonega and their legislature passed laws to take this land from Cherokees. In fact, Carney notes on his timeline of "Native American Education in the United States," that the Cherokees took the state of Georgia to court in 1831, but essentially lost when tribes were defined as "sovereign but 'dependent' nations."[28] Interestingly enough, the famous orator Edward Everett, who delivered the "other" Gettysburg Address on the same day as Lincoln, defended the Cherokees before Congress by attacking the removal bill on May 19, 1830 citing the major problems as the fact that previous removals were voluntary but this one would be forced, that no one even knew if the Western lands would be a suitable area for relocation, and that "acculturation was working." The House pushed the bill through by refusing to recognize but a few opponents and by keeping extremely long hours in an attempt to exhaust the opposition.[29] In the end, Cherokees saw their land raffled off before they could even "remove their belongings from their homes."[30] In a visit to the Cherokee Heritage Center June of 2014, the Trail of Tears rooms include life size sculptures of men, women, and children struggling on the Trail of Tears and an entryway that shows the long bayonets used to force people from their homes without mercy, sometimes without being allowed to even put their shoes on.

In 1830 President Andrew Jackson pressured Congress to pass the Indian Removal Act and the Cherokees were able to negotiate with the American government for several years before they were forced onto the Trail of Tears in 1837.[31] In 1836, the famous American poet Ralph Waldo Emerson wrote a letter to President Martin Van Buren to protest the removal of the Cherokees, pointing out that a few Cherokee had been allowed to represent the whole people and the vast majority did not wish to be removed. In fact, when the impending removal was reported in their newspapers, Emerson writes:

> In the name of God, sir, we ask you [President Van Buren] if this be so. Do the newspapers rightly inform us? Man and women with pale and perplexed faces meet one another in the streets and churches here, and ask if this be so. We have inquired if this be a gross misrepresentation from the party opposed to the government and anxious to blacken it with the people. We have looked at the newspapers of different parties and find a horrid confirmation

28. Carney, *Native American Higher Education*, 158.

29. Reid, *Edward Everett*, 44.

30. Mihesuah, *Cultivating the Rosebuds*, 13.

31. Ibid., 34.

of the tale. We are slow to believe it. We hoped the Indians were misinformed, and that their remonstrance was premature, and will turn out to be a needless act of terror.

Most importantly, he clearly pointed out the moral problems with removing Native Americans from their land, writing "You, sir, will bring down that renowned chair in which you sit into infamy if your seal is set to this instrument of perfidy; and the name of this nation, hitherto the sweet omen of religion and liberty, will stink to the world."[32] In 1838 and 1839, about twelve thousand Cherokees walked what would retroactively become known as "The Trail of Tears."[33]

While it is important to remember that two of the three factions of Cherokees did not walk the Trail of Tears, with one faction relocated willingly to Indian Territory, it is still remarkable that the Cherokee Female Seminary opened a little over a decade after the Trail of Tears. Also, the Cherokee Female Seminary became an impressive architectural example of Native American schooling in Tahlequah, Oklahoma when it was founded in 1851.[34] The Cherokees hired an architect from Boston to build the male and female seminaries, and the large brick buildings boasted Greek columns on three sides. Impressively situated at the top of a hill, each were out of place in Indian Territory—much nicer than seen anywhere else in the state.[35] As the "second oldest institution of higher learning west of the Mississippi River," historians Faulk and Welge claim that it "is deeply rooted in the traditions and culture that were brought to the Tahlequah area by Cherokees who crossed the Trail of Tears in the 1830s."[36] This would make sense since it was that faction of Cherokees, of the three that had so recently been united after coming over on the Trail of Tears, that were most responsible for founding the school.

The Seminary, sometimes referred to as the Park Hill Seminary since that was where it was located, opened in 1851 but closed in 1857 due to a lack of funding.[37] Twenty-six women graduated in 1855 and 1856 out of the forty-five students attending.[38] It was reopened several years after the

32. Emerson, "1836 Letter to President Van Buren."
33. Mihesuah, *Cultivating the Rosebuds*, 13–14.
34. Ibid., 26.
35. Ibid.
36. Faulk and Welge, *Oklahoma*, 308. Faulk and Welge claim the opening date is 1846.
37. McCullagh, *The Teachers*, 11.
38. McCullagh, "The Closing," 50.

Civil War in 1872 and burned down on Easter Sunday (April 10) in 1887.[39] Historian McCullagh quotes the reaction by a Mrs. R. L. Fite: "In a few short hours all that was left of the boast and pride of the Cherokees was its smoking ruins, its fallen walls and its blackened pillars—the end had come to dear old Park Hill Seminary!"[40] "The Honorable William Potter Ross" said, "I shall not forget with what deep regret I beheld its smoldering ruins, its fallen walls and blackened columns, and still more, its homeless inmates and distressed teachers as they were grouped in squads on the ground in the midst of remnants saved from the disaster."[41] The new building was built a few miles up the road in Tahlequah and was dedicated May 5, 1889 with a prayer spoken in the Cherokee language, an address by Chief Joel B. Mayes, and a dinner that followed a program of other speeches and music.[42]

When it opened, teachers at the Cherokee Female Seminary were probably white since Mary Lyon's Mount Holyoke (in Massachusetts) supplied the new seminary with teachers, as Mihesuah explains. McCullaugh wrote that women from the east came to teach at the seminary: "Ellen R. Whitmore, Sarah Worcestor, Harriet Johnson, Pauline Avery . . . Lois W. Hall, and the last principal, Charlotte E. Raymond, and her two assistant teachers, Mary L. Jones and Eliza Jane Ross."[43] Of all of these, only Eliza Jane Ross was Cherokee.[44] Perhaps out of a desire for Cherokee teachers, instead of attending the Cherokee Female Seminary, several Cherokee women were educated at Mount Holyoke during that time. They valued it for its curriculum as well as for its missionary training, a goal the tribe had for educating Cherokee women.[45] As a tuition-free institution, girls had to pass tests to gain entry into the four year program at the Cherokee Female Seminary.[46]

---

39. McCullagh, "Mayme Jane Starr," 478.

40. Ibid.

41. Ibid.

42. Ibid., 479.

43. McCullaugh, "Eliza Jane Ross," 236.

44. Ibid.

45. Mihesuah, *Cultivating the Rosebuds*, 27.

46. Ibid., 30.

The Curriculum

Students studied "geometry, Greek history, intellectual theology," "algebra, physiology, Latin, and Watt's *Improvement of the Mind*."[47] Students also studied "geography," "vocal music," and "advanced arithmetic," but Mihesuah notes that they did not study Cherokee culture.[48] She recounts the prejudice mixed bloods demonstrated toward full bloods in her history, an indication of the extent to which assimilation fractured the tribe.[49] As any gardener knows, the adoption of the name "Rose Buds," was representative of the adoption of the desire to be "cultivated" and assimilated.[50] As any student of women's history knows, the metaphor comparing young women to flowers is one of the most prevalent to be found in Euro-American women's literature in the nineteenth century.

The *History of the Cherokee Indians* offers this schedule:

Students rise . . . 5:30

In Study Hall . . . 6:00–7:00

Breakfast and detail . . . 7:00–8:30

Chapel . . . 8:30–9:00

Recitations 9:00–12:00

Noon . . . 12:00–2:00

Recitations . . . 2:00–4:00

Military drill [probably only performed at the Male Seminary] . . . 4:15–4:45

Supper . . . 5:00

Study Hall . . . 6:45–8:45

First retiring bell . . . 9:00

Second retiring bell . . . 9:15 [51]

47. Ibid., 31.
48. Ibid.
49. Ibid., 39.
50. Ibid., 37.
51. Starr, *History of the Cherokee Indians*, 232.

Emmett Starr, a Cherokee himself who authored an often-referred to history originally published in 1921, also lists the courses taken in the "Preparatory Department":

> First year: Penmanship, Phonetics, Reading, Object Lessons, Grammar, Geography, Arithmetic. Second year: Penmanship, Reading, Object Lessons, Composition, Phonetics, Arithmetic, Geography. Third Year: Penmanship, Reading, Object Lessons, Composition, Phonetics, Arithmetic, Geography.

Courses taken in the "Academic Department" include:

> Freshmen—Ancient languages: Latin, Greek, English; Grammar, Geography, History, U.S. History, Mathematics: Arithmetic, Algebra; Physics, Geography, Physiology.

> Sophomore—Ancient languages, Caesar, Anabasis, English, Rhetoric, History, English History, Mathematics: Algebra, Geometry; Chemistry, Natural Philosophy.

> Junior—Ancient languages: Cicero, Ovid, Thucydides; Modern languages: French, German, English; English literature, American literature, Mental Science, Political Economy, Moral Philosophy, Mathematics: Trigonometry, Analytical Geometry; Botany, Geology.

> Senior—Ancient languages: Virgil, Livy, Homer; Modern languages: Moliere, Goethe; English, Criticism, Mental Science, mental Philosophy, Logic, Mathematics: Surveying and Calculus; Astronomy, Zoology. [52]

The 1951 Centennial Celebration

On May 7, 1951, the Cherokee Tribe celebrated the one hundredth anniversary of the opening of the male and female seminaries, which were later combined into the co-ed institution now known as Northeastern University.[53] Included in the program were two photos of the original female and male seminaries. Following that are photos of two of the female seminary's first teachers, Misses Ellen Whitmore and Sarah Worcester. The celebration began with prayers and included hymns sung in Cherokee, a quartet, a

52. Ibid., 231–32.
53. "One Hundredth Anniversary."

benediction, and a basket dinner.[54] Historian James McCullaugh repeatedly notes the "May Day" celebrations held each year in his various histories of the Cherokee Female Seminary and this celebration was in that spirit. Presented as a play with separate scenes, the theme is listed as "Centennial Celebration of Higher Education in Northeastern Oklahoma," and is followed by "Scene One: Establishment of Seminaries by Cherokee National Council, November 26, 1846." On the left are the names of the original council members and on the right are the names of the individuals playing that role for the scene. On the right, all names are Christianized names, such as Bill Condit and Dow Miller. On the left, the original names show the diversity of the original council with names like James Kell, Pheasant, William Tucker, Oo-soo-ya-duh, Standingdeer, Chu-noo-luh-hus-ky, and Bark Flute, among others.

In direct conflict with the romanticized scenes of what Native Americans were like in the mid-nineteenth century, a decade or so before the Civil War and the emancipation of slaves, the scene recounts the decision to open the seminaries as such:

> Lewis Downing: 'Mr. President . . . I would like to submit the following bill for the consideration of this Council.
> Whereas: At our last session it was recommended by the Honorable John Ross, Principal Chief of the Cherokee Nation,[55] that two institutions of higher learning, one for males and the other for females, be established in the vicinity of Tahlequah; Therefore, be it enacted by the Cherokee National Council, that a seminary for girls be established at Park Hill and one for boys be established near the Ross spring, one and a half miles southwest of Tahlequah.

In the scene, they go on to record a few further statements and the unanimous vote to open the seminaries. "Scene Two: Opening of the Seminaries, May 7, 1851" begins with the "crowning of the May Queen and Promenade." A band played the "Emperor Waltz" and then it was said,

> The school opened with twenty-five young ladies, the flower of the Cherokee Nation as pupils. The large hall and the parlor were

54. Ibid.

55. John Ross, "born near Lookout Mountain, Tennessee, in 1790," was the son of a Scottish father and a mother who was one-quarter Cherokee and three-quarters Scottish. John's name was Cooweescoowee, and although he did not even know the language very well, he rose through the ranks (member of the Cherokee National Council, then president of the council, then co-author of the Cherokee constitution, and then assistant chief) to become chief of the tribe in 1827 (Faulk and Welge, *Oklahoma*, 55).

beautifully decorated; and fragrant with perfume from great bunches of the lovely wild pink azalea or bush honeysuckle. The military band from Ft. Gibson was on hand that day through the courtesy of General Belknap, post commander at that time. The exercise of the day included a most entertaining performance— the crowning of a May Queen . . . it was a beautiful ceremony; the distant music was heard, and as the sound came near a troop of young ladies appeared all in lovely light dresses, escorting their queen, singing as they marched and gathered round the throne— a bower of vines and flowers; and the maid of honor places the crown of lovely roses on her head. In the afternoon when the exercises in the house were over, the band stationed themselves out in the shady Blackjack woods back of the building, and the company, ladies and gentlemen in pairs, promenaded round and round to the music of the band to their hearts' content.

"Scene Three: A Seminary Assembly" included four women and two men to play the roles of the teachers. The original teachers were: Miss Ellen Whitmore, Miss Sarah Worcester, Miss Jane E. Ross [related to Chief John Ross], Miss Florence Wilson, Reverend Thomas Van Horne, and Mr. O. L. Woodford. A note of the program states that the numbers performed by the small group of young women who accompanied the teachers in this scene were drawn from the original program. It begins with a "Recitation" of "Ode to Sequoyah," then moves onto a "Vocal solo" of "Kathleen Mavourneen," a "Composition" called "Scenery" which was "written at the Female Seminary at Park Hill by Miss Lizzie Meigs," a "Piano Solo" of "Dolores Waltz," and ends with a "Duet" of "Juanita." "Scene Four: Recreation, A Play Party" is done by "Indian students," but no explanation follows outside of a short list of the names of the boys and girls who played those roles and their director, a Mrs. Martha Markham. "Scene Five: Oration, 'A Century of Educational Achievement,'" was read by Billy Cooper and is worth recording since this rare primary text captures something that modern scholarship simply does not—the heartfelt love for a distinctly Cherokee history:

> You have just witnessed demonstrations of the marvelous progress made by the Cherokee people up to the beginning of the century just now closing. The invention of an alphabet,[56] the establishment

56. Sequoyah, who was only part Cherokee, invented an 85 or 86 letter alphabet, "each representing a sound in the tribal language" and presented it to the tribal council in 1821. It only took the Cherokees a couple of years to master it, printing books and newspapers in their own language (Faulk and Welge, *Oklahoma*, 51). Later, missionary Samual Austin Worcester ran a printing press at Park Hill (where the seminary was

of a National newspaper, the perfection of a rather perfect system of public schools, either the first or among the first of its kind in the world, the acceptance and practice of the Christian religion and more particularly, the establishment of these two great institutions of higher learning; I repeat that all of these accomplishments indicate marvelous advancement indeed for a people who were at that time less than a century removed from barbarism.[57]

Despite the troublous factionalism that developed among the Cherokees over the problem of removal [the Trail of Tears] and the serious difficulties that arose out of it, the good sense and wisdom of the leaders soon triumphed over the baser elements, and chaos and fratricidal strife were soon transformed into order and cultural growth.[58]

No sooner was progress again on its way than the War between the States [the Civil War] enveloped the Cherokees and reopened the old sores of factionalism and made them even worse than they formerly were.[59] Then, with the days of reconstruction and the advent of the railroad, came the white intruder, and the Cherokees soon found themselves confronted with the problem of tribal dissolution. But regardless of all these apparently insurmountable obstacles the wise Cherokees persisted in holding their heads above the chaotic waves of materialism and courageously pressed on toward the accomplishment of their high educational and cultural ideals.

Soon after the war their two National schools were revived and enlarged, and thus they continued to stand out as a beacon light until statehood. It was largely through the influence of these two schools that the Cherokee people, though greatly outnumbered by

---

located) and published the *Cherokee Phoenix* partially in the syllabary of Sequoyah, as well as the *Cherokee Almanac*, and parts of the Bible (ibid., 79).

57. This statement directly counters the pathos of the Native American cultural revival of the 1960s. Instead of regretting a loss of culture, here it is celebrated. Indeed, this historical piece makes its clear which elements of history the Cherokees chose to treasure and which they chose to leave behind.

58. Chapter 4, "Indian Republics in a New Land," describes how the Cherokees were "split into three factions" after being forced into Indian Territory: "the Old Settlers" who had first moved to Arkansas and then to Indian Territory, the "Treaty Party" who had gone west voluntarily, and the "Ross Party" who had traveled on the Trail of Tears. After a "bloody struggle," the Ross Party obtained power, but it would take the Treaty of 1846 to finally bring the factions together (Faulk and Welge, *Oklahoma*, 73–74).

59. One Cherokee is worth noting here. Stand Watie (Degadoga or "He Stands") "led the Confederate Cherokees during the Civil War, rising to the rank of brigadier general of the Confederate Army" (ibid., 73–74).

outsiders, have been able to hold their own in the new state of Oklahoma [1907] and exert a political and social influence among their competitors far beyond their numerical strength.

A baser people might lose themselves in the crass material-ism of the day and forget their noble heritage of the past, but not so with the Cherokees. These annual homecomings of the old seminaries students, their children, and their friends are, within themselves, indicative of pride and esteem with which they hold these institutions of their earlier creation. These meetings tend to keep alive the memory of the noble traditions established in the past century—traditions that are eternal in their value.[60]

It is fortunate indeed that the First Legislature of Oklahoma recognized this fact by converting the Cherokee Female Seminary into the Northeastern Normal School [i.e., a teacher training school] and by this act helped to perpetuate the Cherokee tradi-tion of enlightenment and progress and pass it on to the coming generations of northeastern Oklahoma. Out of this Normal School grew the Northeastern State Teachers College and then Northeast-ern State College as it is today.

From the one classical and artistically constructed Cherokee building that tops the eminence to our rear, with its ivy-mantled walls, its quaint architectural designs, and its Romanesque towers, the Northeastern of today has grown into a magnificent school plant of some fifteen or twenty buildings, several of which are unsurpassed in design, workmanship, and utility.[61] Besides this, three other structures of the latest architectural design and ar-rangement are well on their way toward completion.

Despite our human tendency, however, to place great stress on buildings and equipment, the inherent worth of all these educa-tional institutions for the past century does not lie in the material equipment but I the higher ideals of life and service that have been instilled in the hearts and minds of this enlightened citizenship of northeastern Oklahoma. As great as has been the achievement of these noble institutions of the past century, may we confidently

60. In the context of this speech, this alludes to the traditions associated with higher education.

61. At first, the institution took a very natural turn toward educating women as teachers, but after World War II, it became a "comprehensive state college, adding liberal arts and master's degree programs to the curriculum lineup." Supported by a local sales tax, the institution was given the opportunity to expand. Buildings for science and athlet-ics went up. The optometry school, known for being the only college in the nation to be allowed to perform laser surgery, is now a major draw for prospective students (Faulk and Welge, *Oklahoma*, 308).

look forward to a period of still greater accomplishment in the century that is now beginning [i.e. the next one hundred years of the institution]. We stand at the threshold of greater problems and greater opportunities. As we look back with pride to the century that is past, may we look forward with hope and expectancy to the one that is to come.

Ending with "Auld Lang Syne," the centennial celebration commenced, leaving to us a rare, complex, and picturesque artifact of American history.

Becoming a Normal School

As a final note on this section, the Five Civilized Tribes Museum in Muskogee, Oklahoma also listed the Cherokee Baptist Academy, but no information was to be found on this institution. Also, the 125th anniversary of the Cherokee Female Seminary was recently celebrated on Northeastern's campus on May 7, 2014 and historian Dr. Brad Agnew provided a history of the institution on the website. In this history, he describes how the seminary became a normal school in the early twentieth century and how it was the only building available for classes for about twenty years. In his short history, he offers many details about the school, including how students used to camp out around the institution during the summers when they came to obtain teacher certification. He wrote:

> Housing students would have been a problem if enrollment had been larger, but with only 180 students, many of whom lived in Tahlequah, accommodations for the entire school were arranged at homes within the town. In the summer, enrollment swelled with the influx of teachers who needed to maintain their certification. Because of the shortage of housing in the summer and their modest means, many students chose to camp on the grounds in tents. Within a few years Northeastern provided tents at $15.25 for the spring or summer term. The school paper declared the campground the most "glorious place . . . in the state for summer camping." To save money many of the students cooked their meals over campfires. Years later, Dr. T.L. Ballenger, a professor of history, recalled, "We could almost tell whether they had bacon for breakfast or not by the way they smelled when they came to class." [62]

---

62. Agnew, "Seminary Hall Narrative."

Historian James McCullaugh records the first summer normal school session as June 4, 1900 with about 140 participants. Twenty-two African American teachers attended a normal school at the "Colored High School" which was located a few miles away.[63] Since many Cherokee once owned slaves, many of these teachers were Cherokee citizens, the descendants of Freedmen. Different certificates were issued, with Class A certificates indicating the teacher had passed several tests with a high score, with Class B indicating the teacher had past most of the tests "omitting algebra, physiology, and civil government," and Class C being given to any teacher fluent in both Cherokee and English.[64] These teachers could teach in schools where the students were full bloods. The last session was held in 1908.[65]

Finally, two memorials were erected on the campus and for many years they flanked a walkway until one had to be moved. The first memorial was a column built in 1914 and dedicated to "Ann Florence Wilson, principal teacher at the Cherokee Female Seminary between 1875 and 1901." In 1919 one was added for John Ross.[66] On a visit to NSU recently, the dedications actually attached to them attribute one to the memory of the male seminary and one to the memory of the female seminary.

Conclusion

Visiting Tahlequah and seeing NSU and the Cherokee Heritage Center revealed just how important the Cherokee Female Seminary was. At the Cherokee Heritage Center, visitors can walk up and view the three remaining columns of the first seminary and the bases of several columns. At NSU, visitors can stand in the circular courtyard just in front of the seminary building, now used as office space for administrators, and read about a variety of Cherokees who have been significant to the tribe and its history. In the center of the courtyard was a statue of Sequoyah. On the drive back to Oklahoma City, the beauty of its rolling hills, winding roads, and forests of trees added to the feeling that within Tahlequah was a remarkable community of people who had overcome great challenges to achieve all that they had. A poem written by a Cherokee woman, Mrs. Lena Harnage Adair,

63. McCullaugh, *The Teachers*, 37.

64. Ibid., 43.

65. Ibid., 55.

66. Agnew, "Seminary Hall Narrative."

called "Tahlequah" attempts to capture its beauty and the accomplishments of her people:

> Here's to Tahlequah with her wooded hills / Her sparkling springs and tinkling rills, / Her rocky cliff by fern o'ergrown, / And her shady nooks by lovers known . . .
> Here Sequoyah, the Cadmus, his alphabet brought, / Which with infinite patience and skill he wrought; / Schools were established to teach the youth, / And churches, to spread Christianity's truth.[67]

In conclusion, while this chapter is but a brief sketch of an institution and its people, it is important enough to be added to any inclusive history of women's education in the United States and it is further evidence that the myths of the American West were just that—clever mixes of truth and fiction that were used to perpetuate prejudice so long as some segment of society could benefit from it. Most importantly, it is a little-known stepping stone on the road to social justice for women that is worth exploring in more detail.

---

67. Starr, *History of the Cherokee Indians*, 333.

8

Educating the Chickasaws, Choctaws, and Other Tribes

The Chickasaws: Bloomfield Academy

THE MISSIONARY JOHN CARR opened Bloomfield Academy as a boarding school for girls in 1852.[1] His second wife was the teacher. Like the Cherokee teachers, she too had been educated at Mount Holyoke.[2] The Bloomfield Seminary for Indian Girls opened with twenty-five students.

Cobb also notes that Bloomfield Academy had a full curriculum and Christian leadership. Like the Cherokees, the Chickasaw eventually rejected the missionaries, but not Christianity. Cobb explains that the Superintendent was to be of "the highest moral character, or Christian standing," and students had to read well, be familiar with the New Testament, and be of "good moral character."[3] The curriculum included "logic, chemistry, astronomy," "botany," "spelling, reading, writing, arithmetic, geography, English grammar, U.S. history, physiology, rhetoric, civil government, natural philosophy, general history, algebra, and American literature."[4] Referred to as the "Bryn Mawr of

1. "Bloomfield Academy," http://www.okgenweb.org/schools/county/chickasawnat/bloomfield.htm.
2. Carr, "Bloomfield Academy," 366–79.
3. Cobb, *Listening to Our Grandmother's Stories*, 53.
4. Ibid., 58.

the West," Cobb notes that Bloomfield graduates were known as "Bloomfield Blossoms" because of their excellent reputation.[5]

Cobb states it opened in 1852, but a firsthand account says it really began to accept students in 1853 as a boarding school.[6] In the words of Sarah J. Carr (third wife of the missionary John Carr who founded the school), recorded in a 1924 edition of *The Chronicles of Oklahoma*, the school had much to offer:

> The girls were taught if necessary the English language and the alphabet; spelling, reading, writing and arithmetic, both mental and written, and, as they advanced, natural philosophy, grammar, "Watts on the Mind," botany and history of the United States during the regular school hours. The opening morning session was at half past eight and continued with a recess until half past twelve. The older pupils studied from five to six in the afternoon. Before this, in the afternoon they were taught to cut, make and mend their own clothes. They were also taught how to do all the ordinary house work, cooking excepted. The older pupils were taught each Saturday in the pastry department Instruction in all these domestic duties was required by the contract. The division of labor was after the plan adopted at Mt. Holyoke Seminary, and never seemed irksome to anyone. In the afternoon at stated hours they were taught needle, wax, worsted and coral work, also drawing, painting and vocal music. In each of these departments they showed taste and made fair proficiency. The departments of fancy work and music was taught by [the second] Mrs. Carr.[7]

Girls began the day with a scripture they had memorized, then engaged in singing, then went to "Sabbath school" to learn about the Bible, and then heard the missionary in charge, Mr. Carr, preach.[8] Even though the schools were for Native Americans, it also served the whites who lived among them. Sarah gives a partial list of the girls who first attended the school:

> I will here give the names of some of the older girls who first entered the school. Serena and Lorena Factor, twins, daughters of full blooded Indians [sic]. Rebecca Burney, daughter of a deacon of the Cumberland Presbyterian Church. Rebecca Colbert, sister of Frank Colbert who built the bridge across Red River. Amelia and

---

5. Ibid.

6. Carr, "Bloomfield Academy," 369.

7. Ibid., 369–70.

8. Ibid., 370.

Lucy Kemp, daughters of Jackson Kemp. Mary and Frances Kemp, daughters of Joel Kemp, who owned the ferry. Mary Ann Colbert, daughter of Morgan Colbert, deacon in Cumberland Presbyterian Church. Alice Warner, daughter of Dr. Warner. She married Captain Welch, of the Confederate army. Mary Reynolds, whose parents resided in the neighborhood. Elvirn and Elzira Colbert, daughters of Lemuel Colbert and Carter Elzira Hoyt. Others were: Emily Allen, Sallie Shecho and Mildred Fletcher.[9]

Like many Native American institutions, it closed in 1861 because of the Civil War. However, in 1876, the Chickasaw legislature provided for that a female seminary be held there again. "The plan for both schools," according to the OK Gen website, "called for forty-five students between the ages of nine and eighteen who were able to read well in *McGuffey's Fifth Readers*, spell well, and read in the New Testament, and be of good moral character. Only one child from a family would be received and no pupil would be allowed to remain longer than five years." Like other Native American schools, it was taken over by the government in 1899. It burned down in 1914 and was relocated from Achilles, Oklahoma (south of Durant) to Ardmore.[10]

The Choctaws: Wheelock Academy

As historian Catherine Colby notes, Oklahoma has the largest Native American population of any state, with over 100,000 brought in as a result of the 1830 Indian Removal Act.[11] Those who survived the journey formed the Five Civilized Tribes. These consist of the Choctaw, the Cherokee, the Chickasaw, the Creek, and the Seminole. However, it was the Choctaw who gave Oklahoma its name through the suggestion of their chief, Allen Wright. "Okla Homma" means "home of the red man." The Choctaw are also known for having the first constitution written within Oklahoma's borders, written in June of 1834.[12]

According to Dennis Miles, several academies for Choctaw girls opened in the 1840s. He writes:

9. Ibid., 373–74.

10. "Bloomfield Academy." http://www.okgenweb.org/schools/county/chickasawnat/bloomfield.htm.

11. Colby, "Wheelock Academy."

12. Ibid.

The Treaty of Dancing Rabbit Creek, signed in Mississippi in 1830, stipulated that the Choctaw were to remove west of the Arkansas Territory and that this land would become their permanent home. The tribe struggled to survive after arrival, but by the mid-1830s missionaries were developing neighborhood schools for the Choctaw children. To further the work of educating their youth, in 1842 the Choctaw General Council enacted a law that established six boarding schools: Spencer Academy, Fort Coffee Academy, Koonaha (Kunaha or Sunsha) Female Seminary, Ianubbee (Ayanubbe) Female Seminary, Chuwahla (Chuwalla) [The Oklahoma History Center lists it as Chuala] Female Seminary, and Wheelock Female Seminary. Fort Coffee Academy was divided into a male and a female branch in 1845. The latter, located five miles southeast of Fort Coffee, was called New Hope Seminary. In addition, Armstrong Academy was established in 1845 near present Bokchito in Bryan County, and Norwalk Academy was opened in 1846 near Wheelock Seminary as a boarding school for boys. These institutions were originally run by missionaries, but by the 1890s those that remained were operated by educated Choctaws.[13]

The Five Civilized Tribes Museum in Muskogee, Oklahoma also listed Tuskahoma Female Academy, dedicated December 1891, and Tamaha. The Oklahoma History Center lists Iyanabi Female Academy; also listed in an article published in *Chronicles of Oklahoma*.[14] The Choctaw Academy in Kentucky is described as being the first national school for Native Americans, but it was for boys.[15] While the Choctaw inhabited Alabama, Mississippi, and Georgia, this school was established by Colonel Johnson, who served as Vice President of the United States in 1837, and described as successful for producing men who held "prominent positions in the county," with many becoming preachers.[16]

My husband's maternal grandmother went to school at Wheelock Academy as a child in the 1920s. Ella Anna Garrison Mowdy's delayed birth certificate lists her as Choctaw, born January 16, 1920 in Pernell, Oklahoma. Pernell is south of Oklahoma City, east of Lawton. The U.S. Department of the Interior's Bureau of Indian Affairs lists her as 3/8 degree Choctaw and her mother, Isabelle Pernell Garrison, as 3/4 Choctaw. He remembers her describing the way the school teachers would punish students

13. Miles, "Choctaw Boarding Schools."

14. Davison, "Oklahoma's Educational Heritage," 354–72.

15. Foreman, "The Choctaw Academy."

16. Dunham, "The Choctaw People"; Miles, "Choctaw Boarding Schools."

for speaking in their own language, but also her feelings of disappointment when she could no longer attend school after the eighth grade.

Like many, she was a mixed blood who married into white culture, but she is also representative of the ways that she had a foot in both worlds. For example, when he was a child, Jerry remembers her singing hymns to him in her native language. She taught him some of the language as well, something he remembers as part of his childhood but didn't know well enough to keep as part of his adult life. From what I can derive from the scraps of history that address this phenomenon, a temporary engagement with these dying languages is common. Ella devoted herself to her home and to cooking meals from scratch. Her husband was a preacher and she was a housewife, enjoying life in their tiny wooden home right off the railroad tracks in McAlester, Oklahoma. In many ways, she was like other women who were expected to stay home. She probably valued the opportunity to fit into society by living out the 1950s ideals associated with motherhood and homemaking, ideals with roots deep in American culture.

In conclusion, built around 1832, Wheelock Academy was the example school for over thirty schools built by the Choctaw and other tribes in Oklahoma. In 1842, it became the first Choctaw National Academy and other tribes used it as a model as well. It closed in 1861, as all Choctaw schools did, because of the Civil War.[17] Colby notes that the school had a reputation for "academic excellence."[18] While there, girls studied "natural philosophy, algebra, astronomy, history, Greek, and Latin," but in 1932, it became a "regular Indian school," a place to send the underprivileged to.[19] Like so many others, Wheelock was destroyed by fire and rebuilt. The fire occurred in 1869 and the rebuilding in 1890 and 1894, so it is easy to imagine that by the 1920s and 30s when Ella Mowdy attended, the school was sufficiently run down enough to be handed over to students used to expecting little in life.[20] Even so, no matter the state of the buildings they learned in, the Native American seminaries for educating girls and young women were bright spots against the pastoral backdrop of rural Oklahoma.

17. Colby, "Wheelock Academy."
18. Ibid.
19. Ibid.
20. Ibid.

The Seminoles: Emahaka Mission

Seminoles were once part of the Creeks, but became their own tribe when some of them moved to Northern Florida.[21] Despite resistance, Chief Holahte Emathla led the first group to Oklahoma in 1836. According to Frank, "By 1839 most of the Seminole had been relocated west. By 1842 they numbered about 3,612 in the Indian Territory. There they eventually formed the Seminole Nation of Oklahoma. A minority of the Seminole (between 350 and 500) remained in Florida." After being forced to go to Oklahoma, they were put under the governance of the Creeks, but established a nation in 1856. Yet, in 1898, all of their lands were divided and subsequently lost due to fraud.[22]

According to Pamela Koenig, this troubled tribe was first educated through The Oak Ridge Mission, established in 1848. It was a Presbyterian institution and the first Seminole boarding school. Later came the Wewoka Mission, the Mekusukey Academy for boys, and the Emahaka Mission. These schools demanded that children not speak Muskogee and did as much as possible to erase their cultures.[23] At the Oak Ridge Mission, a manual labor school, boys and girls were educated by Presbyterian missionaries who educated their children there as well. The school was destroyed in the Civil War.[24] According to Koenig, "The Methodist Episcopal Church built Sasakwa Female Academy in 1880 near Sasakwa. In 1887 the Seminole took control of the school and Chief John Jumper hired William Packer Blake as superintendent. In 1892 the institution was moved south of Wewoka and later consolidated with a new girls' boarding school called Emahaka Mission or Academy."[25]

Emahaka Mission (a Seminole word that means "girls'" school) was established in 1894 near Wewoka. There, up to 112 girls could learn anything from math to foreign languages. "To be admitted," Koenig writes, "girls had to be between the ages of six and eighteen, and their band chief had to guarantee their 'good moral character.'"[26] Oklahoma historian Robert E. Trevathan interviewed Byron Blake, a man who remembered attending

21. Frank, "Seminole."
22. Ibid.
23. Ibid.
24. Koenig, "Seminole Schools."
25. Ibid.
26. Ibid.

this girls' school between 1894 and 1897 in an article he published in *The Chronicles of Oklahoma*. Because Byron's father was an assistant engineer at the academy, he was allowed to attend classes there.[27]

To begin, Byron described the school itself. While one might imagine a wooden structure, the typical schoolroom in a building that doubled as the church on Sundays, this was not the case. Instead, Byron recalled a brick and stone structure, four stories high in the center, with "spacious porches on two triple storied wings that were accentuated by turrets on the southeast and northeast corners." Built with a cost of $50,000, it copied the architecture of the Mekasukey [Mekusukey] Academy, the boys' school. Students lived on the third and fourth floors and had hot and cold running water, steam heat, fireplaces, and indoor bathrooms. The infirmary was on the third floor as well. The classrooms were on the main floor, with the music room furnished with several pianos. The kitchen, laundry, and dining room were in the basement. Bryon's uncle was hired by Baptist preacher and former principal chief of the Seminoles, John Jumper, to be the Superintendent.[28]

Historian Robert Trevathan writes that Bryon recalled befriending the only other boy, the son of a cook who worked there, and remembers being ill-treated by the girls who surrounded them. However, he still remembers his teacher, Miss Prickett, because she gave him a barlow knife for Christmas that he carried for years afterward. Byron also remembers how he was in danger once when a group of young Seminole boys rode up, "shooting sixguns," to impress the young girls at the school.[29]

To illustrate how frightened he was of the Seminoles, Bryon offers us a story. Before he lived and went to school among the Seminoles, the one thing Bryon knew (from the stories his grandpa told him) is that Native Americans "scalped" white people.[30] So, as he rode the train to his new home, he worried about this danger most of the way—except when he stopped in Guthrie and Oklahoma City and the excitement took his attention for the moment. After they stopped at the train depot in Purcell, Byron was sent to fetch milk for his baby sisters. He went out on foot to the store in the deep cold of winter. He was relieved to make it there and back without seeing a single "Indian," but by the time he returned to the train depot,

27. Trevathan, "School Days," 265.
28. Ibid., 266.
29. Ibid., 267.
30. Ibid., 268.

his hands were frozen from carrying the cold, metal milk can. Hurrying inside to get warm, he froze in fear. Inside, six or more "dark skinned, black haired men" were warming their hands by the stove. Terrified, Bryon stood there, door open behind him.[31] The biggest one among them came over, shut the door, picked him up, and set him in front of the stove. In his words, "The Indian pried my fingers from the bail of the milk can and took both my freezing hands and began rubbing them in his long hair, making huffing noises like a buffalo." Amused by the memory, Bryon remembered that "his face was right against mine," and he "melted" with fear.[32] However, the rest of the article describes his life among the Seminoles, full of fond memories and love for them.

Unfortunately, this school burned in 1927 after combining with the Mekasukey [Mekusukey] Academy in 1911.[33] Instead of the impressive array of curriculum enjoyed by white female academies, students took care of animals and learned basic skills, all of them in English. It closed in 1930.[34]

Like many other Native American tribes, many Seminoles embraced Christianity. Mekasukey means both "where the chiefs meet" and "where Christianity is taught."[35] In particular, the Baptists and Methodists have remained popular among Seminoles in both Oklahoma and in Florida, but adopting Christianity has not resulted in them giving up their culture. Frank writes, "Many Seminole Christians frequently participate in the stomp dance, green corn ceremonies, traditional fasts, and other ancient rituals. Although English is the predominant language in Oklahoma, many of the Christian hymns are still sung in the traditional Muskogee language."[36]

The Creek Teacher's Normal School

Very little information on the Creek Tribe could be found, even on the Creek Tribe's website for the nation. However, Clyde Ellis fills in a few gaps: "In the Creek Nation the Presbyterians opened Koweta Mission School in 1843 and Tullahassee Mission Boarding School in 1850. The Methodists opened Asbury Mission School the same year." In addition, "the American

31. Ibid.
32. Ibid., 269.
33. Koenig, "Seminole Schools."
34. Ibid.
35. Ibid.
36. Frank, "Seminole."

Baptist Home Mission established Indian University in 1885 in Muskogee on 160 acres of land donated by the tribe. Renamed Bacone College in 1910, it continues to serve Native students."[37] Also, in the historical papers of Alice M. Robertson, made available online by the University of Tulsa, she is listed as the Supervisor of Creek Schools in Muskogee, Indian Territory and writes about a meeting to be held for the "Creek Teacher's Normal School." Those in attendance would receive training or be tested for teaching certificates since the government had appropriated funds to meet the demand for teachers in the area.[38] The Five Civilized Tribes Museum also listed Eufaula Boarding School and the Spaulding Female Seminary. It is my hope that additional information may one day become available if there is anything to add to this brief account.

Other Tribes

The Oklahoma History Center lists Koonshaw Female Seminary and Sasakwa Female Academy, but additional information was not available. In western Oklahoma, tribes did not open their own schools.[39] Clyde Ellis sums up what tribes did in Oklahoma who were not one of the Five Civilized Tribes. "At the Kiowa-Comanche-Apache (KCA) Reservation . . . the Friends (Quakers), Catholics, Baptists, and Methodists sponsored day schools and boarding schools beginning in the 1870s." In 1871, two Quakers from Ohio opened a boarding school for Caddoes and Wichitas living near Fort Sill. "It later became the Fort Sill Indian Boarding School and served mainly the Comanches and Apaches." The same year the Quakers also opened the Wichita School (later called Riverside Boarding School) north of Anadarko.[40]

According to Ellis:

> Father Isidore Ricklin opened St. Patrick's Boarding School at the Anadarko Catholic mission in 1892; like the Wichita School, it was taken over by the Bureau of Indian Affairs (in 1911) and renamed the Anadarko Boarding School. The Kiowas got their own school in 1893 when the Rainy Mountain Boarding School opened south of Gotebo, more than twenty-five years after the Medicine Lodge

37. Ellis, "American Indians and Education."
38. "Alice M. Robertson."
39. Ellis, "American Indians and Education."
40. Ibid.

agreement had promised them schools. In addition to these, the federal government operated an off-reservation boarding school at Chilocco in north-central Oklahoma between 1884 and 1980. Of these, only the Riverside School remains in operation today. Rainy Mountain closed in 1920, St. Patrick's in 1963, and Fort Sill in the 1970s.[41]

Also, after Native Americans lobbied for better schools, "In 1934 the Congress enacted the Johnson-O'Malley Act, authorizing the federal government to contract with states to provide educational services for Indians. Since 1994 Title IX, a federal education act for American Indians, Native Alaskans, and Native Hawaiians, has provided funds to school systems specifically for Indian education."[42]

Conclusion

As I am part Cherokee myself (according to family lore since none of my ancestors signed the Dawes or Miller rolls), these histories are truly interesting to me. Hidden beneath my green eyes and Scottish-Irish features is the same ancestry that many native Oklahomans share. Today, the Five Civilized Tribes are held together by tribal newspapers and cultural events. As a member of the Choctaw Tribe, my husband receives a newspaper periodically, as well as a calendar and a beautiful ornament each Christmas. These are pleasant reminders of cultural ties. Today, each tribe has a website hosted by their nation, and those who can claim membership enjoy a variety of benefits. Yet out of the five tribes, only the Cherokee and the Chickasaws have had recent work done on the histories of the female seminaries. The Oklahoma Centennial Celebration in 2007 inspired many new histories, some of which capture pieces of tribal history. It is my hope that the work of scholars, using histories and archival materials that are present because of the diligence of the Oklahoma Historical Society, will continue to grow.

41. Ibid.
42. Ibid.

9

Women Stepping Out of the Home Sphere and Into the Teaching Profession

Training Teachers

JAMES W. FRASER'S *PREPARING America's Teachers: A History* reveals that at first teaching was considered a temporary profession, not a lifelong career.[1] Young women might teach a year or two before marriage, and men might take on teaching while waiting for a better opportunity to present itself. Barbara Solomon claims that "economic necessity, religious zeal, and intellectual curiosity drew women into school teaching" and although "Joseph Emerson in Massachusetts, Noah Webster and Jedidiah Morse in Connecticut, and John Poor and Benjamin Rush in Pennsylvania supported female education, it was women who made the greater contributions in ensuring the permanence of female institutions and in raising their standards."[2] Indeed, the women who started the most influential female seminaries also can be credited with shaping teaching before Horace Mann's normal schools and before Henry Barnard's Teachers' Institutes swept the nation in an effort to bring quality, oversight, and, most especially, systemization to teacher training.[3]

1. Fraser, *Preparing America's Teachers*.
2. Solomon, *In the Company*, 17.
3. Fraser, *Preparing America's Teachers*, 61.

Emma Willard and Troy Female Seminary
(Established 1821), Troy, New York

While the female seminaries did not offer a course in pedagogy as they did in the normal schools, by following the advice of men such as James Carter and Edward Everett,[4] Emma Willard was the first to intentionally prepare teachers at Troy Female Seminary, opened in 1821.[5] Troy was quite different from other female seminaries because it had a curriculum that was much like the ones found at male colleges.[6] Willard, unlike other women who had chosen to leave teaching after marriage, had spent about two decades teaching by the time she opened Troy, so she had a great deal of experience to draw upon when she created the "Willard system" that was designed to educate women to the same levels as men were (although not for the same vocations), especially when they were going into the teaching profession. In the system, students first learned the materials, then recited them from memory, and then taught the subjects to each other.[7] Willard also built a network called the Willard Association for the Improvement of Teachers. This network resulted in about 150–200 schools that were modeled on hers and were dedicated to teacher training for women.[8]

A brief look at Emma Willard's educational background shows that although she was born in 1787 as the sixteenth of seventeen children, she was fortunate enough to have brothers who banded together to pay for her to learn in the school of the Patten sisters in Hartford and then later in a school by Mrs. Royse at the Academy of Berlin.[9] Afterwards, she attended an academy led by Thomas Miner, a Yale graduate and a physician, and also one at Hartford.[10] Although the education women could receive in her time was not equal to that of men, by all accounts she overcame its limitations and became a gifted teacher. At seventeen, she was the mistress of Kensington (a summer school), then a teacher in the Academy of Berlin, and then she was offered no less than three positions to teach: in Westfield, Massachusetts;

---

4. Ibid., 53.

5. Ibid., 31–32.

6. Ibid., 31.

7. Ibid., 32.

8. Ibid., 33.

9. Goodsell, *Pioneers of Women's Education*, 17.

10. Ibid., 17; Woody, *A History of Women's Education*, 1:344–345.

in Hudson, New York; and in Middlebury, Vermont.[11] She chose to go to Westfield, beginning a path as an educator and women's advocate that would characterize her exceptional life. In 1814, Emma began a boarding school in Middlebury to help her husband who had met with recent financial troubles, and by doing so came to recognize how flimsy and weak the education most girls were receiving at other boarding schools really was.[12] It was here that she began to work on her famous "An Address to the Public; Particularly to the Members of the Legislature of New York, Proposing a Plan for Improving Female Education," which she would present to the New York legislature in the hope of obtaining funds for a female seminary.[13]

After finishing her plan, she left for New York in 1818, but when she addressed the New York Legislature in 1819, her plan failed miserably. Yet she did gain the approval of President Monroe, Thomas Jefferson, and even John Adams.[14] In terms of leadership and teacher preparation, Willard articulated much of what Horace Mann would just a couple of decades after her when he called for systematic teaching training. Also, in her plan, she argued against the most common type of schooling available to women at that time—the boarding schools. Run by any woman who cared to open her home to boarders, these schools operated without libraries, trained teachers, and oversight by qualified leaders. They were dependent upon profits from students, and the girls left there with "toys" (artifacts of an ornamental education in the arts) and not knowledge. For example, she wrote:

> It is for the interest of instructresses of boarding schools, to teach their pupils showy accomplishments, rather than those, which are solid and useful. Their object in teaching is generally present profit. In order to realize this, they must contrive to give immediate celebrity to their schools. If they attend chiefly to the cultivation of the mind, their work may not be manifest at the first glance; but let the pupil return home, laden with fashionable toys, and her young companions, filled with envy and astonishment, are never satisfied till they are permitted to share the precious instruction.[15]

Instead of that kind of education, Willard argued that young women should be taught in places that employed a variety of teachers, each

11. Goodsell, *Pioneers of Women's Education*, 17–18.
12. Ibid., 20–21.
13. Ibid., 21.
14. Ibid., 24.
15. Willard, "An Address to the Public," 10.

well-trained in her subject, just like at male institutions. She wanted the young women to receive instruction from women for the same reason voiced in most arguments for women's education: propriety. At the time, instruction from men was believed to allow room for moral compromise. She wanted qualified leadership and state funding so that the best minds held oversight positions, thereby raising the quality of education and so the schools would no longer depend on emphasizing their entertainment value and could focus instead of emphasizing the acquisition of knowledge. Instead of being the "satellites of men," women would be trained to center their lives around God.[16] Echoing Mary Wollstonecraft, a British woman who published *Thoughts on the Education of Daughters* in 1796 and who was widely noted as an early feminist who also argued for equal rights and opportunities for women, Willard capitulated that, of course, women should make themselves "agreeable" to men, but since men were not perfect and God is, then why should women try to live up to the standards set by those who are merely human?[17] She argued:

> The errour [sic] complained of, is that the taste of men, whatever it might happen to be, has been made a standard for the formation of the female character. In whatever we do, it is of the utmost importance, that the rule, by which we work, be perfect. For if otherwise, what is it, but to err upon principle? A system of education, which leads one class of human beings to consider the approbation of another, as their highest object, teaches, that the rule of their conduct should be the will of beings, imperfect and erring like themselves, rather than the will of God, which is the only standard of perfection.[18]

Finally, drawing on themes of Republican Motherhood, she claimed the state should be responsible for educating mothers in order to continue the propagation of civic ideals necessary for the continuance of the new country.[19]

16. Ibid., 15.

17. Wollstonecraft, *Thoughts on the Education of Daughters.*

18. Willard, "An Address to the Public," 15.

19. Ibid., 16.

Raising the Standards

It is worth bringing a bit of Willard's "plan" to light in a little more detail as it set goals for female education by echoing some arguments already being made while offering arguments of her own that would help shape education for women. Enormously influential, her plan sought to raise standards for female education by offering well-organized, rational arguments. It should not be mistakenly thought of a feminist manifesto, however. Although educating women eventually allowed them to achieve equality, in this plan, Willard quickly stated that she was not arguing that women should be educated the same as men "as the female character and duties" are different from a male's in order to avoid rejection of her plan based on an ideology that challenged social norms.[20] However, she went on to argue that by "raising the female character" the whole community is improved, especially because women's primary role is that of mother, again couching her argument in the dominant ideology of the day.[21]

Willard began her argument with a brief outline: "I. Treat of the defects of the present mode of female education, and their causes. II. Consider the principles, by which education should be regulated. III. Sketch a plan of

20. Ibid., 5.

21. Ibid., 6. Willard echoes Benjamin Rush's argument in "Thoughts Upon Female Education" when he argues that Americans must leave behind British arguments against female education because life is different in the United States. Women should be educated because:

III. From the numerous avocations to which a professional life exposes gentlemen in America from their families, a principal share of the instruction of children naturally devolves upon the women. It becomes us therefore to prepare them, by a suitable education, for the discharge of this most important duty of mothers.

IV. The equal share that every citizen has in the liberty and the possible share he may have in the government of our country make it necessary that our ladies should be qualified to a certain degree, by a peculiar and suitable education, to concur in instructing their sons in the principles of liberty and government.

V. In Great Britain the business of servants is a regular occupation, but in America this humble station is the usual retreat of unexpected indigence; hence the servants in this country possess less knowledge and subordination than are required from them; and hence our ladies are obliged to attend more to the private affairs of their families than ladies generally do of the same rank in Great Britain. "They are good servants," said an American lady of distinguished merit in a letter to a favorite daughter, "who will do well with good looking after." This circumstance should have great influence upon the nature and extent of female education in America.

a female seminary. IV. Shew [sic] the benefits which society would receive from such seminaries."[22]

One of the biggest problems with education for women was its leadership. Willard wrote:

> Civilized nations have long since been convinced that education, as it respects males, will not, like trade, regulate itself; and hence, they have made it a prime object to provide that sex with everything requisite to facilitate their progress in learning: but female education has been left to the mercy of private adventurers; and the consequence has been to our sex, the same, as it would have been to the other, had legislatures left their accommodations, and means of instruction, to chance also.

She went on to argue:

> Education cannot prosper in any community, unless, from the ordinary motives which actuate the human mind, the best and most cultivated talents of that community, can be brought into exercise in that way. Male education flourishes, because, from the guardian care of legislatures, the presidencies and professorships of our colleges are some of the highest objects to which the eye of ambition is directed. Not so with female institutions. Preceptresses of these, are dependent on their pupils for support, and are consequently liable to become the victims of their caprice. In such a situation, it is not more desirable to be a preceptress, than it would be, to be a parent, invested with the care of children, and responsible for their behavior [sic], but yet, depending on them for subsistence, and destitute of power to enforce their obedience.[23]

To sum up her argument, while the best educated and most experienced men competed for leadership positions in male educational institutions, women who were little qualified could easily assume leadership in institutions they began on their own—without the benefit of experience or of a proper education.

As mentioned earlier in the summary of her plan, Willard also argued for women to be trained as teachers because in society because it was most proper that women by taught by women: "Feminine delicacy requires, that girls should be educated chiefly by their own sex. This is apparent from considerations that regard their health and conveniences, the propriety of

22. Willard, "An Address to the Public," 7.
23. Ibid., 7–8.

their dress and manners, and their domestic accomplishments."[24] While contemporary readers might object to the absurdity of the claim, it is important to remember that women did not have the same legal rights as they do today. Also, by arguing that women learn best from women, Willard shrewdly justified a proper education for women while making arrangements for their protection as well.

In the second part of her argument, Willard illustrated that male students were educated at the proper time and for a proper length of time. In contrast, female students were hurried through boarding schools and return home with little more than stories of amusement.[25] While arguments abounded about the different abilities of men and women, Willard pointed out it was not necessarily a difference in ability, but in the way they were instructed. While male students were allowed time to absorb knowledge, female students were not.

Wrapping up this section of the argument, she offered an argument rooted in ideals associated with Republican motherhood:

> It is the duty of a government, to do all in its power to promote the present and future prosperity of the nation, over which it is placed. This prosperity will depend on the character of its citizens. The characters of these will be formed by their mothers; and it is through the mothers, that the government can control the characters of its future citizens, to form them such as will ensure their country's prosperity. If this is the case, then it is the duty of our present legislators to begin now, to form the characters of the next generation, by controling [sic] that of the females, who are to be their mothers, while it is yet with them a season of improvement.[26]

In the next section of her argument, Willard described an ideal plan for how a female seminary should be instituted. First, it should be in a permanent building, not in a person's home.[27] It should have a library, a governing board, and suitable instruction in these four areas: "1. Religious and Moral. 2. Literary. 3. Domestic. 4. Ornamental." She stated all teachers should be required to teach and uphold religious and moral instruction. She also wanted them to offer "literary" instruction, but she meant more than literature. This term, in her day, included the sciences as well. In addition

24. Ibid., 8.
25. Ibid., 12–13.
26. Ibid., 16.
27. Ibid., 17.

to the sciences, the term meant they should teach philosophy and history, as well.[28] She argued for teaching standard practices in the domestic arts, and then explained that they should be taught for practical purposes and not allowed to consume the majority of a student's time at school as they did at boarding houses.[29]

In addition to these suggestions, Willard added that an institution must be governed by a specific set of rules, that admissions standards should be set, that expectations for achievement be established (and punishment for those who don't achieve should follow), and that a specific length of time and an established program be offered for their studies (in contrast to the common practice of jumping from one "school" to another to learn this art or another).[30] She suggested issuing a certificate upon graduation, but is careful to note that she did not mean that this certificate should be used to allow women to speak publicly, as that was offensive at the time. This certificate would only be awarded after students passed rigorous examinations, some of which would include performances, and surprisingly, despite the denouncement just made of women speaking publicly, they would be performed for both men and women spectators. Further, she suggested that students study for three years and be admitted at no younger than fourteen years of age.[31]

In the very last section of her argument, "Benefits of Female Seminaries," Willard offered a story:

> Counting on the promise of her childhood, the father had anticipated her maturity, as combining what is excellent in mind, with what is elegant in manners. He spared no expense that education might realize to him, the image of his imagination. His daughter returned from boarding school, improved in fashionable airs, and expert in manufacturing fashionable toys; but, in her conversation, he sought in vain, for that refined and fertile mind, which he had fondly expected. Aware that his disappointment has its source in a defective education, he looks with anxiety on his other daughters, whose minds, like lovely buds, are beginning to open. Where shall he find a genial soil, in which he may place them to expand? Shall he provide them male instructors? —Then the graces of their persons and manners, and whatever forms the distinguishing

28. Ibid., 18–19.
29. Ibid., 22.
30. Ibid., 24.
31. Ibid., 25.

charm of the feminine character, they cannot be expected to acquire. — Shall he give them a private tutoress? She will have been educated at the boarding school, and his daughters will have the faults of its instruction second-handed. Such is now the dilemma of many parents; and it is one, from which they cannot be extricated by their individual exertions. May not then the only plan, which promises to relieve them, expect their vigorous support.[32]

In providing a story, Willard used the same technique Hannah Foster's used in her *Letters of a Preceptress*, but Willard's story led readers to draw exactly the opposite conclusion.

As she drew her plan to a close, she reiterated some of the points made earlier, but with additions important for my discussion of women entering the teaching profession since she addresses this vocation specifically. One point already made was that the female seminaries should have admissions standards and trained teachers, but here she added that having these teachers meant they could free men from this occupation to seek the kinds of employment which women could not.[33] Also, she argued that educating women as teachers would improve education in the common schools.

The efficacy of the argument for women to be educated because of the virtues of Republican Motherhood cannot be overstated. Willard went on to say that "It is believed, that such institutions, would tend to prolong, or perpetuate our excellent government. An opinion too generally prevails, that our present form of government, though good, cannot be permanent. Other republics have failed, and the historian and philosopher have told us, that nations are like individuals; that, at their birth, they receive the seeds of their decline and dissolution."[34] Thus, as a new country, Willard suggested that they use education to ensure its future existence.

Willard went a little further than this argument, though. Without an education, she claimed, women would make the mistakes of the past, indulging themselves in greed. Since women should submit to men, Willard argued, it was therefore their fault that when women failed morally. Education was needed to avoid these errors.[35] Other benefits would be that women would learn to react with reason, not emotion, that they would be taught religion and morality, that they would value higher forms of cul-

32. Ibid., 26–27.
33. Ibid., 27–28.
34. Ibid., 29.
35. Ibid., 30–31.

ture by partaking in them themselves, that "housewifery" would become an interesting endeavor through real attention to it as an area of study, that students would become educated in more than "show and parade" by a genuine acquaintance with "moral and intellectual pleasures," that they would become better mothers and moral guides for their children, and, finally, she argued:

> And surely, there is that in the maternal bosom, which, when its pleadings shall be aided by education, will overcome the seductions of wealth and fashion, and will lead the mother, to seek her happiness in communing with her children, and promoting their welfare, rather than in a heartless intercourse, with the votaries of pleasure: especially, when with an expanded mind, she extends her views to futurity, and sees her care to her offspring rewarded by peace of conscience, the blessings of her family, the prosperity of her country, and finally with everlasting happiness to herself and them.[36]

Willard ended her plan with a rousing argument for women's education, once again showing her plan was rooted deeply in the ideologies of Republican Motherhood:

> In calling on my patriotic countrymen, to effect so noble an object, the consideration of national glory, should not be overlooked. Ages have rolled away; —barbarians have trodden the weaker sex beneath their feet; — tyrants have robbed us of the present light of heaven, and fain would take its future. Nations, calling themselves polite, have made us the fancied idols of a ridiculous worship, and we have repaid them with ruin for their folly. But where is that wise and heroic country, which has considered, that our rights are sacred, though we cannot defend them? that tho' a weaker, we are an essential part of the body politic, whose corruption or improvement must affect the whole? and which, having thus considered, has sought to give us by education, that rank in the scale of being, to which our importance entitles us? History shows not that country. It shows many, whose legislatures have sought to improve their various vegetable productions, and their breeds of useful brutes; but none, whose public councils have made it an object of their deliberations, to improve the character of their women. Yet though history lifts not her finger to such an one, anticipation does. She points to a nation, which, having thrown off the shackles of authority and precedent, shrinks not from schemes of improvement, because other nations have never attempted them; but which, in

36. Ibid., 31–33.

its pride of independence, would rather lead than follow, in the march of human improvement: a nation, wise and magnanimous to plan, enterprising to undertake, and rich in resources to execute. Does not every American exult that this country is his own? And who knows how great and good a race of men, may yet arise from the forming hand of mothers, enlightened by the bounty of that beloved country, — to defend her liberties, — to plan her future improvement, — and to raise her to unparalleled glory?[37]

As strong as her plan was, it failed. After her plan was not accepted, she moved from Middlebury to Waterford, New York to set up her school in 1819 and again Governor Clinton tried to secure funding for her, but failed.[38] She went to Troy in 1821 because the Common Council of Troy raised four thousand dollars for her school, and at the age of only thirty-four, she ran an advanced seminary that was wildly popular, drawing students from other states.[39] Troy Female Seminary became profitable within ten years and offered a wide array of subjects, such as "mathematics, science, history, logic, and domestic and finishing school studies such as art and music."[40] Finally, besides influencing the shift from boarding schools to seminaries, she funded the tuition for women who wished to teach, asking that the school be repaid from their new teacher's salaries, making it possible for more women to join the profession.[41]

She also led the way in the creation of curriculum since she had to create many of her own teaching materials, and she won a medal at the World's Fair of London in 1851 for her "time-maps" called "Temple of Time" and *Chronographer of Ancient and English History*.[42] Emma earned quite a bit of income from the books she wrote, and she used them to train teachers although her vision was, in her own words, to teach the "broad sphere of woman's duties and accomplishments."[43] Referred to as the "Vassar College of New York," Troy helped the American public to understand the value of women's education.[44] It is notable for being the first girls' seminary in the

37. Ibid., 34–35.
38. Goodsell, *Pioneers of Women's Education*, 25.
39. Ibid., 28.
40. Martina, "Emma Hart Willard," 942.
41. Fraser, *Preparing America's Teachers*, 32.
42. Woody, *A History of Women's Education*, 1:346.
43. Ibid.
44. Ibid., 1:347.

United States to offer advanced courses in "algebra and geometry, history, geography, and nature philosophy (physics)."[45] Although she did not get as far as Catharine Beecher in some respects, she was absolutely instrumental in passionately pushing ahead a woman's right to an equal education by taking the idea of the female seminary just as far as it could possibly go in her time. She is also notable to setting the pace for teacher education and for working hard to win a place for women to work by suggesting that men enter other fields.

Catharine Beecher and Hartford Female Seminary (Established 1823), Hartford, Connecticut

Catharine Beecher, after starting the Hartford Female Seminary in 1823, also decided about ten years later that teaching should be a primarily female profession.[46] At Hartford, Catharine Beecher and another teacher worked together to teach almost every subject without even the benefit of separate classrooms for the different ages or a board to draw upon.[47] After fighting against the chaos of having such a diverse group of students together and against the stress of trying to cover too much material in too little time with too few resources, they built a new building with all of the needed resources and covered more content over a longer period of time.

Beecher gave "special lectures" on being a good student and a good Christian.[48] Each of the teachers in the new building only taught two or three subjects as opposed to a wide variety and one person had the job of simply enforcing the rules in all of the classrooms, sort of like a school principal of today. The challenges of educating women included not having the needed materials to train those she hired to teach them, and a serious lack of funds to cover teacher pay, much less the ongoing demand for some needed resources. She also had to take on all of the administrative tasks, including teaching.[49] She left in 1833.

However, her career continued. After making Hartford a teacher education school, she opened the Western Female Institute in Cincinnati in 1833 and spent several years in the 1840s traveling and speaking to argue

45. Goodsell, *Pioneers of Women's Education*, 29.

46. Fraser, *Preparing America's Teachers*, 36.

47. Woody, *A History of Women's Education*, 1:352–53.

48. Ibid., 1:353–54.

49. Ibid., 1:355.

that women should be prepared to teach out west.[50] Gathering support from Horace Mann, Henry Barnard, and Samuel Lewis, she was successful in raising funds and in starting the National Popular Education Board. Through this board, it was Beecher who ran teacher training institutes for a month and who placed teachers across the country who would agree to at least a two year commitment to their new schools.[51] According to Fraser, Troy sent out about 600 teachers between 1839 and 1863, the National Board about 600, most of Mount Holyoke's graduates entered into teaching, and a small number of Ipswich graduates entered teaching as well. Until 1850, the female seminaries had the most impact on the teaching profession—much more so than the normal schools.[52] These seminaries altered the definition of the nineteenth century "True Woman" ideal as well. With Catharine so vigorously claiming it as part of a woman's sphere, she added to the idea that women should be pious, pure, obedient, and skilled in domesticity by also asserting that women were "strong, courageous, self-sufficient, rational, assertive, and above all, intelligent."[53]

Just two years after leaving Hartford, Catharine published "An Essay: Education of Female Teachers" that is worth drawing upon here.[54] This important text, currently only available on microfilm, is just as important as Willard's "Plan." Pointing out many of the same problems Willard did, Catherine begins her essay by pointing out the central problem with education: "Communities seem almost entirely dependent upon chance, both for the character and the perpetuity of schools. If good teachers stray into their bounds, they are fortunate; if poor ones, they have no remedy."[55] She goes on to cite a problem still plaguing our public schools and higher institutions today. "There needs to be added a well devised plan of government . . . in such a way that the removal of any one teacher does not interrupt the entire system of instruction."[56] In other words, we need some sort of uniformity in how students are taught. We need to be able to remove teachers without their removal destroying the institution. While at the time, she was referring to continuity in an intellectual sense, today we can add

50. Fraser, *Preparing America's Teachers*, 37–38.

51. Ibid., 38.

52. Ibid., 41.

53. Ibid., 42.

54. Beecher, "An Essay."

55. Ibid., 3.

56. Ibid., 4.

it in terms of a financial sense because the cost of removing ineffective teachers is astronomical.

Like others, Beecher capitalized on the argument that the reason we must educate women is that these same women educate the children. She wrote, "What is the most important and peculiar duty of the female sex? It is the physical, intellectual, and moral education of children. It is the care of their health, and the formation of character, of the future citizen of this great nation."[57] She justifies all education, both ornamental (such as needlework) and traditional (such as rhetoric) in light of women's needs for excellence as mothers, as housewives, and as Christians. She claims that memorizing facts is only a small part of education. "Other pursuits are designed for the cultivation of certain mental faculties, such as *attention, perseverance,* and *accuracy.*"[58]

For rhetoric, she says it results in the cultivation of "taste and imagination," a valid claim since Hugh Blair's 1787 *Lectures on Rhetoric and Belles Lettres* was widely used in a variety of both male and female institutions to improve the communication skills of students. However, while the title may seem to indicate that the book was to teach students to appreciate the beauty of language, it was a lengthy text that went much farther than that. In it, Blair taught the basics of rhetoric by drawing upon classical scholars, such as Aristotle, and he taught the most important thing there is to know about the responsible use of persuasion: that it is about allowing the hearer or reader to adjust their beliefs according to their own wills, not about attempting to control those one attempts to persuade.[59] As a widely popular text in the nineteenth century, it encapsulates a sense of moral direction that values free will. While educators continue to shape the "mental habits and general character of the pupils,"[60] as Beecher writes, Beecher's argument was to "strengthen religious obligation," not to undermine it.

Like Willard, Beecher wanted libraries and adequate resources for women.[61] She wanted the Bible as the standard rule for moral instruction. "All agree that the Bible is the true standard of right and wrong," she wrote, "and the only rule of faith and practice. All agree that the evidences of its divine authority should be understood, and that its contents should be

57. Ibid., 5.
58. Ibid., 7; italics original.
59. Bradford, "The Older Rhetoric Revisited."
60. Beecher, "An Essay," 8.
61. Ibid., 9.

studied."[62] In her time, she imagined that she was perhaps ahead of her peers by explicitly arguing against any one religious sect being able to dominate instruction on the Bible; most educators of her time never imagined that it would not only be completely eliminated from our public schools but be subjected to wide-spread denigration in our universities. Echoing today's arguments, Beecher wanted excellent teacher preparation ("three years in preparing for such duties") and small class sizes ("one teacher is furnished for every ten pupils through the nation").[63] Her suggestion is that at least "two or three seminaries for female teachers" be created and for each "a model school" be provided for the practice of teaching.[64] By having all teachers trained at a limited number of institutions, she argued that they would be uniformly prepared. "When female teachers are well trained for their profession, a great portion of the higher female schools will be entrusted to their care, and they will be prepared to co-operate in propagating a uniform and thorough system of female education, both intellectual and moral."[65] Closing out her argument, which was delivered at the 1835 meeting of the American Lyceum, she again calls for the public funding of institutions for the higher education of women.[66] Her ideas, her arguments, and her textbooks were enormously influential in shaping education in her time and leaving a valuable legacy for those who would follow.

Mary Lyon and Mount Holyoke Female Seminary (Established 1837), South Hadley, Massachusetts

Zilpah Polly Grant used the same scholarship system as Emma Willard did at the Ipswich Female Seminary, located in Massachusetts. Yet her influence was not as great as that of Mary Lyon. Mary Lyon's (1797–1849) education at Byfield changed her life. There she learned from Joseph Emerson, who once trained for the ministry at Harvard, and was mentored by Zilpah Grant, who was a few years her senior. After working with Grant for about a decade as a teacher, the next major figure in teacher education, she left Ipswich to found Mount Holyoke in 1837, using public funds.[67] In fact, Mary opened

62. Ibid., 12.
63. Ibid., 15.
64. Ibid., 19.
65. Ibid., 20.
66. Ibid., 21.
67. Fraser, *Preparing America's Teachers*, 34.

Mount Holyoke Female Seminary in 1837 after collecting gifts of money, the first school ever to be opened by these means.[68] She was still forced to offer the teachers low pay, however. Students had to do their own domestic work, although domestic work was not formally taught as a subject.[69]

She had around 12,500 students over the years, most becoming "teachers, home makers, and missionaries."[70] Building on Willard's curriculum, she added that her curriculum be as long as that required of men. She also launched an effective job assistance program for her graduates, demanding decent salaries and an assurance of a known job location.[71] It was her teachers that were so strongly sought by the Native American female seminaries in what would one day become Oklahoma. Following the teaching of Joseph Emerson, Mary thought teachers should also be missionaries.[72] As "missionary-educators," women were sent to the West and to the South as "cultural and civilizing influences."[73] In fact, deploying women as both teacher and missionary served three purposes:

1. to teach;

2. to be a "cultural and religious" missionary on the frontier;

3. to find someone to marry.[74]

In a circular dated June 10, 1835, Lyon draws a clear connection between education and Christianity stating the seminary was to be "under the guardianship of those who are awake to all the interests of the church" and that "It is to be based entirely upon Christian principles . . . to cultivate the missionary spirit among the pupils; the feeling that they should live for God, and do something as teachers."[75] She goes on to ask that the church donate money to the institution. In a circular addressed to her friends in 1836 she wrote, "This work of supplying teachers must be done or our country is lost, and the world will remain unconverted."[76]

---

68. Woody, *A History of Women's Education*, 1:359.

69. Ibid., 1:360.

70. Ibid., 1:361.

71. Fraser, *Preparing America's Teachers*, 35.

72. Melder, "Mask of Oppression," 38.

73. Ibid.

74. Ibid., 39.

75. Lyon, "Inception of Mount Holyoke," 19.

76. Ibid., 24.

Lyon's legacy is acknowledged in Helen Horowitz's history of the "Seven Sister" colleges that came later. Vassar and Wellesley used the same system of discipline that Lyon had used; Wellesley's founder, Henry Fowle Durant, attempted to recreate Mount Holyoke entirely on his estate outside of Boston.[77] In fact, he only hired women to fill positions at his new college.[78] Its influence is clear. Horowitz writes, "Mary Lyon created Mount Holyoke to turn daughters who were acted upon into women capable of self-propelled action." To accomplish this, Lyon "drew together key elements: academic subjects to train the mind as an instrument of reason; domestic work and a carefully regulated day to meet material needs and to protect health; a known, clear sequence to each day to lend order and predictability; a corps of transformed teachers who provided proper models for imitation; and a building shaped like a dwelling house as the proper setting for study, prayer, work, and rest."[79] Seventy percent of its graduates went on to be teachers and two led two of the Seven Sisters, namely Vassar and Wellesley.[80]

In a collection of letters written between 1831 and 1837 and currently only available on microfilm, the formation of her ideas regarding education can be seen. In 1831, she wrote the trustees of the Ipswich Female Seminary this letter:

Gentlemen:

You doubtless recollect that in September, 1829, a committee from your board was appointed to inquire what was necessary to secure the continuance of our school in this place.

The first requisite is a seminary building free of rent, containing a hall of sufficient size to accommodate one hundred and seventy-five scholars, several recitation rooms, a laboratory, a room for a library, and a reading room. The second requisite is a boarding house, completely furnished, for one hundred and fifty boarders, to be contiguous to the seminary building, and surrounded by a few acres of playground.

The care of the conduct of the scholars, and the general internal arrangements of the house, must devolve on the teachers. The

77. Horowitz, *Alma Mater*, 4.

78. Ibid., 5.

79. Ibid., 12.

80. Ibid.

pecuniary affairs of the establishment should be committed to an agent, appointed by the trustees, to whom he should be responsible.

Yours, very respectfully,

Z. P. Grant
Mary Lyon[81]

In this letter, Lyon clearly outlines what she believes is needed to effectively run an institution of higher education. In a letter written to a Professor Hitchcock in 1832, she outline four goals for a female seminary:

1. To increase the number of well qualified female teachers.

2. To induce many who have already become teachers to make further improvement on their education.

3. To exert an influence in bringing as much of the labor of instruction into the hands of ladies as propriety will admit.

4. To lead the way toward the establishment of permanent female seminaries in our land. That there are no seminaries of this kind is, we believe, a fact.[82]

What is most interesting about the goals she sets is that she echoes the sentiments of Beecher: Education belongs in the hands of women.

In conclusion, more than any others, Willard, Beecher, and Lyon have provided the greatest amount of influence on the empowerment of women because they fought the hardest to establish institutions for the higher education of women and to provide women with an acceptable profession— that of teaching. By proving themselves in this profession, women were able to successfully break down barriers to other lines of work. To sum up, it was the emphasis on providing a Christian education to children at home and to students in the public schools that won women the right to higher education and the Christian roots of women's rights should not be dismissed or diminished.

81. Lyon, "The Inception of Mount Holyoke College," 5.
82. Ibid., 7.

10

From Seminaries to Normal Schools: Farmville Female Seminary

From Seminaries to Normal Schools

WILLARD CLAIMED TO HAVE "sent forth from Troy two hundred trained teachers before one was graduated from a public normal school in this country."[1] The normal schools had all that she had argued for in 1819—state funding, qualified leaders, and a stringent curriculum. In addition to this, they incorporated courses in pedagogy as well. The story of the normal schools begins in Massachusetts in 1837. That year, Horace Mann was elected as the first secretary for the new Board of Education in the United States.[2] Mann quickly started the *Common School Journal* and used it to spread his six principles of education:

1. Citizens cannot maintain both ignorance and freedom;

2. This education should be paid for, controlled, and maintained by the public;

3. This education should be provided in schools that embrace children from varying backgrounds;

4. This education must be nonsectarian;

5. This education must be taught using tenets of a free society;

1. Fraser, *Preparing America's Teachers*, 33.

2. "Horace Mann." http://www.biography.com/people/horace-mann-9397522.

and

6. This education must be provided by well-trained, professional teachers.[3]

Known as the "Father of the Common School," his work in Massachusetts, which won a free public school education for children using taxpayer funds, was imitated in other states.[4] Because of Horace Mann, normal schools opened for teacher training. In fact, he was a critical part of the opening of the very first school for teacher training; it opened in Massachusetts in 1838.[5] Horace Mann gave both women and children access to greater opportunities than they had ever dreamed. In his final commencement speech, he said, "I beseech you to treasure up in your hearts these my parting words: Be ashamed to die until you have won some victory for humanity."[6] Indeed, he dedicated his life to bettering others'.

Case in Point: Longwood Female Seminary

The development of Longwood University, which began as the Longwood Female Seminary back in 1839, is a good representation of the evolution of teacher education in the United States at other institutions. In addition to its place in history as a female seminary turned normal school, Longwood is the heart of Farmville, Virginia, located within an hour's drive of Appomattox where the Civil War officially ended. Farmville is known for being a battleground for equality where the townspeople once decided to shut down the public schools in the 1950s for five years rather than accept racial integration. As a mix of new and old, Farmville is a place of outdoor movies where residents bring their lawn chairs and blankets and watch old classics projected onto the remains of an old building, of "First Friday" summertime celebrations held on a big stretch of grass next to the Appomattox River where kids might kick around a soccer ball or jump in the bounce house or dip their feet in the river. It is a place of quaint stores full of furniture and antiques, and it is a place of skinny pine trees lining winding, hilly roads that reach far into the country. In many ways, Longwood captures the rural and

---

3. Ibid.
4. "Horace Mann (1796–1859)."
5. Ibid.
6. "Horace Mann." http://www.biography.com/people/horace-mann-9397522.

the urban because of its rural location and local culture in combination with the urban influences brought in by the professors who teach there.

When I (Kristen Welch) was an assistant professor in the English Department at Longwood, I remember walking down "Brock Commons," a central throughway on the small campus, and noticing a historical marker describing the early days of Longwood. In grainy photos, women wearing long dresses posed in front of the school. These students of Farmville Female Academy were intriguing to me and I wondered how Longwood University came to be.

As the story goes, in 1839 seven investors purchased an acre of land using shares of stock and began to build what would be Longwood.[7] In 1842, the building was completed and it was time to open the doors. Back then, it was a growing town, located on the Appomattox River, which was important because it provided a way to transport tobacco and other goods easily. It was also a railroad stop between Richmond and Lynchburg. The investors surely knew of schools like Troy Female Seminary, Hartford, and Mount Holyoke and expected a similar degree of success with their endeavor. Just down the road, Hampden-Sydney, an all-male college (and one of only three remaining in the U.S.), had been open since 1776 and had sent several of its graduates to Princeton, evidence that this small town could accomplish much.[8]

At the time it was opened, one advantage Longwood had over other institutions for women was its investors. While many other seminaries struggled with financing, Longwood benefitted from its supporters. Thus, the tiny campus, now home to several buildings and dorms (enough to require a visitor take at least ten or twenty minutes to circle the entire campus by walking briskly), was beautiful in its original state as only one building. This building, looking very much like a colonial house with windows lined up across the front, appeared stately upon a large lawn framed by a picket fence. It offered a "home" atmosphere and an 1859 engraving of the seminary included in Rosemary Sprague's history of Longwood shows it was framed by trees and had a circular drive in front. On the engraving, ladies in bell-shaped dresses are pictured walking around, and two horses gracefully trot in front of the lovely building, carrying a man in a top hat on

7. Sprague, *Longwood College*, 1.

8. Ibid., 2, 3.

one and a lady in a feathered hat and long dress on the other.[9] This pleasant building would last until a fire destroyed it in 2001.[10]

Although it began as a school for women in Farmville in 1839, it was not a normal school (i.e., a teacher training school) originally. Opened two years after Horace Mann successfully argued that future schoolteachers needed to be educated and just one year after he established the country's first normal school in Massachusetts in 1838, the idea for a normal school had no champion yet.[11] However, William Henry Ruffner, known as the "Horace Mann of the South," was given a position as the State Superintendent of Instruction in Virginia in 1869, recommended by General Robert E. Lee himself.[12] Working with Jabez Curry, on March 7, 1884, the Virginia legislature passed a bill Curry had drafted that allowed for the opening of a normal school in Farmville.[13] Today, Longwood has a thriving education department and is perhaps most known for its commitment to training excellent teachers.

Longwood's Christian Roots

At Longwood, my office and the classrooms I used were in Grainger, right on High Street and right next door to the building named after Ruffner, which housed some of the administration and some classrooms. As I walked out the front doors of Grainger, I had two churches in sight. On the right was the Methodist church, pastored by a woman. This church often hosted the Camerata Singers and my young son and I would go to sit in the balcony and listen while they sang *a cappella*. On the left was the Episcopal church, favored by many Longwood faculty for its liberal views. Both churches were quite old and small, having lovely stained glass and a feeling of history in their bones. Of the two, the Methodist church is more historically significant since the female seminary originally "operated under the sponsorship of the Southern Methodist Conference." In fact, for the normal school to be established, it had to be deeded over to the town and from the town to the state because the state could not take over church property.[14]

9. Ibid., 8.
10. Jordan, "Once Upon a Time."
11. "Horace Mann (1796–1859)."
12. Sprague, *Longwood College,* 45, 46.
13. Ibid., 47.
14. Ibid., 48.

Like most seminaries and colleges of the nineteenth century, Christianity was deeply ingrained in the institution. A pamphlet from the 1859–60 school year for the Farmville Female College reveals this particular strand of history.[15] Proverbs 31:30 graces the introductory page: "Favor is deceitful and Beauty is vain, but a woman that feareth the Lord, she shall be praised." Woven throughout the descriptions of the school and its amenities are references to Christianity and to Christian ideals, but in particular, the section on "Religious Instruction" is indicative of its roots:

> The Bible will be employed as the basis of all religious and moral instruction. The religious teachings of the College contemplate a through and harmonious acquaintance with the fundamental facts and truths of Christianity, and while no pains will be spared to impart a practical knowledge of the Christian religion, parents and guardians may rest assured that no attempts will be made to interfere with the particular denominational relations of the pupil.
>
> On the Sabbath the young ladies are expected to attend such place of worship as their parents may designate. In addition to the public services on Sunday, the teachers and pupils will assemble for an hour in the evening for the reading and contemplation of the Scriptures, and also to sing sacred melodies. These Sabbath evening gatherings are among the pleasantest occasions we enjoy, and have a softening and elevating influence upon the character.[16]

Furthermore, a description of the "Daily Exercises" stated that the first hour after waking up would be devoted to prayers alongside the teachers, and that after breakfast there would be an assembly for worship and reading and responding to the Bible.[17] Finally, it is noted on page 11 that "a liberal discount" on tuition is offered to the "children of Clergymen."

The Fourth Annual Catalogue of the Farmville College, dated 1876–77, is quite different but on page 23 the Christian orientation of the college is made clear in the section "Religious Exercises and Privileges."[18] It begins, "We desire and intend to conduct our school under *religious influences,* believing these to be indispensable to a proper education. Christianity and the Holy Scriptures will, always and in all things, be recognized and set forth as of the *highest value, importance, and authority.* Nothing *opposed* to them will be tolerated" (italics theirs). It further says that students will wor-

15. "Farmville Female College."

16. Ibid., 6–7.

17. Ibid., 8.

18. "The Fourth Annual Catalogue of Farmville College."

ship daily, attend Sunday School and church, and attend a weekly prayer meeting. "The conversion and religious improvement of our pupils will ever be regarded as objects of paramount interest."

While little of Longwood's Christian beginnings remain and while the majority of faculty seem to lean more toward secular views, the students are another story and, in my experience, often seemed likely to remain tied to their religious views and cultural ideals even as they reached the end of their studies there. One curious tie to Christianity that remains on the now secular campus is Longwood's patron saint, Joan of Arc. One of Longwood's most popular professors recounts the history of two statues of her that are still on campus to this day:

> The Joan of Arc statue in the Rotunda, which was presented by the senior class of 1914 [Rosemary Sprague credits this to the 1911 graduating class],[19] is a reproduction of the famous one chiseled in 1870 by the French sculptor, Henri-Michel-Antoine Chapu of Paris. He called it "Joan of Arc Listening to the Voices." Today, the original stands in the Museum of Luxembourg in Paris. We in Farmville refer to this famous statue more informally as "Joanie on the Stony."

As for the other statue:

> The equestrian Joan statue in the Colonnades was given in 1927 by the internationally renowned sculptress, Anna Hyatt Huntington. The original of this Joan statue had been completed for Riverside Church in New York City just the year before, and the sculptress, upon hearing of the admiration of the students at the State Teachers College at Farmville for this work, determined to present them with the first reproduction [Rosemary Sprague claims it was the Alpha Delta Rho sorority that requested the copy from Ms. Huntington in 1927].[20] Since its unveiling in Farmville by Mrs. Huntington on April 27, 1927, it has been affectionately called "Joanie on the Pony." This Joan statue originally sat nearer to French Building in the Colonnades than it does now, and you can still see the original location by a mark there on the walkway left from the marble base. On the night of the East Wing Fire in 1949, Joanie on the Pony, unable to be moved from her base, was so close to the fire that she glowed red from the heat of the blaze.[21]

19. Sprague, *Longwood College*, 105.

20. Ibid.

21. Jordan, "Once Upon a Time."

As is common knowledge, Joan of Arc was a young woman who led some of the French in battle against the English. What might not be common knowledge is that Joan was a particularly "pious" child who head voices of the saints speaking to her, but she revered them too much to speak back. It was the voices that compelled her to find a way to participate in the battle in Orleans. Although the history is complex and full of twists and turns, in the end Joan was successful in battle but later captured by the English. After what they considered a fair trial, she was burned at the stake for heresy and for wearing men's clothes on May 30, 1431. The commemoration of her in 1914 would have been timely and meaningful for the all female student body at Longwood because Joan was declared a saint in 1909.[22]

Despite her embodiment of Christian ideals on a decidedly secular campus, Joan of Arc remains a vital part of Longwood University through the Leadership Series as well as a Joan of Arc award given each year to one or more students and therefore might be considered as an important symbol for shaping the character of today's teachers on Longwood's campus. According to the Longwood website, there are three levels in the leadership series: The Shield, the Paldron, and the Gauntlet.[23] These levels are meant to help students see their progress towards good leadership as it builds over time, and the students come to understand that on Longwood's campus, Joan of Arc is synonymous with excellence in leadership. Also, each year students are nominated for high honor of possibly receiving The Joan of Arc Visionary Leadership Award. The recipient must have done something "to achieve a future community of citizen leaders working for the common good of society."[24] Thus, Joan of Arc is still meant to connote self-sacrifice for the common good as well.

Longwood's commitment to Christian education was hardly unique. The ties between education and Christianity propelled women towards a better future, even if the motives included a desire to keep women in their "place." Sweet writes that "throughout the 1830s, 1840s, and 1850s, despite historians' emphasis on the rejection of higher education by evangelicals, many of America's evangelical denominations were competing furiously with one another to give their daughter's the same intellectual training as their sons. With passionate engagement they built female seminaries and

22. "St. Joan of Arc." In *Catholic Encyclopedia*: http://www.newadvent.org/cathen/08409c.htm.

23. Longwood University, "Joan of Arc Leadership Program."

24. Longwood University, "Award Descriptions."

encouraged their members to build them."[25] The trend continued through-out the nineteenth and twentieth centuries, as Dr. Ruelas describes in his book, *Women and the Landscape of American Higher Education: Wesleyan Holiness and Pentecostal Founders.*[26] Because so many Christians valued education, by 1850 the number of literate women was roughly equal to that of men.[27] Indeed, as Lindley describes in *You Have Stept Out of Your Place*, the bridge between social justice and women was often built through religion, not in spite of it.

When it involved the promulgation of Christian values and social mo-res, Thomas Woody explains that the educational goals of the early female seminaries were much like those for the academies.[28] The cultivation of the mind was one key goal, but so was the cultivation of Christian principles. Religious and domestic training were key. While religious training ran the gamut from just observance to missionary work, the "religious zeal" of founders such as "Joseph Emerson, Emma Willard, Zilpah Grant, Catha-rine Beecher, Mrs. Phelps, and Mary Lyon" is well documented.[29] A vast majority of "early seminaries were created by religious organizations," as Woody observes.[30] Contemporary scholar Catherine Clinton echoes this fact when she writes, ""Reading and writing were the primary tool of the 'English Education,' with study of Scriptures a high priority."[31] As a case in point, Longwood University began much the same way many institu-tions of its time did, as a Christian institution that openly desired to attract Christian young women as its students.

The Curriculum: Early Years

Not much is known about the curriculum in the seminary's earliest days. In the beginning, it offered no courses in math or science, sticking to English, Latin, Greek, French, and piano.[32] Yet by 1856, the students were learning "Latin, French, astronomy, chemistry, botany, rhetoric, philosophy, algebra,

25. Sweet, "Female Seminary," 41.

26. Ruelas, *Women and the Landscape.*

27. Sweet, "Female Seminary," 41.

28. Woody, *A History of Women's Education*, 1:397.

29. Ibid., 1:398.

30. Ibid., 1:400.

31. Clinton, "Equally Their Due," 12:13.

32. "Farmville Female College," 8.

grammar, geography, and arithmetic."[33] In a copy of the 1859–60 "Annual Register and Announcement of the Farmville Female College," Geo. La Monte is listed as President and "Professor of Latin, Higher Mathematics, and English Literature."[34] Miss Susan B. Fowler was Preceptress and "Instructress in French and English Branches," Miss M. Millie Gibson was "Instructress in English Branches and Mathematics," Mr. A. S. Simmons was "Professor of Music or Piano and Guitar," Miss Anna M. H. Wood was "Instructress on Piano," Miss Susan B. Fowler was "Drawing and Painting," and Mr. A. S. Simmons is listed a second time with "Vocal, Music, and Organ" credited to him. Under "Course of Instruction," it states:

> The Course of Instruction is intended to develop the intellectual, social and moral faculties, and by imparting a thorough, practical, accomplished and Christian education, fit the pupil for the faithful discharge of the responsible duties of life.
>
> Great pains will be taken to promote the intellectual advancement by rendering the acquisition of knowledge pleasant, and by training the pupil to correct habits of thought and reflection. The proper exercise of the social feelings will be encouraged by inculcating whatever belongs to refined manners and dignified courtesy in our intercourse with others, while reading the Bible will familiarize the mind with the truths of our holy religion, and imbue the heart with right principles of action and rules for government of life.

Two departments are listed: The Preparatory Department and the Collegiate Department. In the Preparatory Department, students could take: "Reading, Writing, Spelling and Definitions, English Grammar, Arithmetic, Geography, History and the simpler forms of composition, etc." In the Collegiate Department, students could take:

> Arithmetic finished, Ancient Geography, English Grammar, Parsing and Punctuation, History of France, Quackenbos' English Composition, Mythology, History of Greece, Elocution, Astronomy, Philosophy of Natural History, Roman and Grecian Antiquities, Analysis of the English Language, English Synonyms, Algebra, History of Rome, Natural Philosophy, Rhetoric, Physiology, Outlines of History, Logic, Chemistry, Geometry, and Geology.

33. Ibid.
34. Ibid.

The Senior Class could take: "Science of things familiar, Karne's Elements of Criticism, Evidences of Christianity, Intellectual Philosophy, English Composition, Theoretical and Analytical Botany, Moral Philosophy, Butler's Analogy, Book-keeping and Forms of Business, and Principles of Taste." Below this list it is noted that "Reading, Writing, and Spelling throughout the course. A pupil entering the Collegiate Department will be classed according to her attainments in the above courses or its equivalent. *Latin* or *one of the Modern Languages* on *one Instrument,* will be required of a candidate for a Diploma." The diploma earned would be called a "Mistress of Arts."

In the Annual Catalogue from 1876–77, there are five instructors listed: Rev. Paul Whitehead, President and "Professor of Moral and Mental Philosophy, and English Literature," John Murray (M.A., University of Virginia), "Professor of Mathematics and Natural Sciences," Edward A. Allen (University of Virginia), "Professor of Languages," Mrs. Virgilia M. Whitehead, "Music," and Miss T. Epia Duncan, "Piano."[35] The Primary and Introductory Department lists Miss Bettie J. Powers as Principal and Miss Rosa M. Duffied, Miss Nannie F. Bradford, and Miss Sarah W. Dalby as Assistants. Miss M. C. Nolley presided over study hall, Mrs. S. G. Stewart over the "Domestic Department," and Miss Mary L. Bernard was "Matron."

A poem published in the 1876–77 Annual Catalogue by a Mrs. Margaret J. Preston titled "A Rhyme for the Annual Celebration of the Margaret J. Preston Literary Society of Farmville College," published June 6, 1876, shows one girl's attempt to change the mindset of her young peers:

> A group of girls let loose from school?
> Caged birds set free in sunny hours!
> Chocked waters bursting bound and rule—
> An upset basket of Spring flowers!
>
> How glad you look! How sweet, how gay!
> In flutter of supreme elation:
> How your young bosoms beat to-day
> With strange and eager expectation!
>
> Why are you glad? Because you're tired
> of pouring over textbook pages,
> And think there's lore to be desired
> Untaught by all the wisest sages?

35. "Fourth Annual Catalogue," 4.

Why are you gay? Because the bands
of school day duty that so bind you,
You disentangle from your hands
And fling with right good will behind you?

Slaves of the clock—you deem you've been
Constrained to learn, eat, sleep by measure:
With leave to go, nor out nor in.
Nor at your own, but others' pleasure.

And henceforth, thro' this summer's shine
I see in every little beauty
Who lifts her brimming face to mine
This written plain—'A truce to duty!'

Oh, darlings! – If you saw it so!
Whether your future gleams or lowers—
The happiest hours your lives will know
Are just these very school-girl hours!

The Change to a Normal School and Its New Curriculum

After it became a normal school in 1884, with Ruffner elected as its principal, the direction changed with the hiring of Celeste E. Bush, a teacher at the Connecticut State Normal School, as vice principal.[36] She taught "geography, physiology, United States history, and 'Morals and Manners,'" while a Miss Gash, who had graduated from Mary Washington College and who had taught at the Tennessee Normal School, taught "English grammar, English Literature, general history, rhetoric, and penmanship." But that was not all. Miss Brimblecomb, a student at the Boston Conservatory and teacher at the Massachusetts Normal School, taught vocal music; Miss Lee taught math, "drawing, bookkeeping, and calisthenics," Mr. Robertson taught "natural sciences, Latin, and algebra;" Miss Johnson taught piano; and Dr. Ruffner taught "psychology, ethics, didactics" and some natural science.[37] Instead of the basics offered in the early days, the students were receiving a robust education after Dr. Ruffner brought about the new vision for the school.

36. Sprague, *Longwood College*, 50–53.
37. Ibid., 54.

Over the years, the curriculum for teachers evolved. Dr. Ruffner wanted a model school where elementary school children would be taught.[38] New teachers could observe an experienced teacher at work and then practice their own teaching techniques. In 1884 the model school was opened and the children of Farmville came "in droves."[39] The new teachers and their students worked hard, but in 1885, a preparatory department was established to address gaps in the education of the new teachers.[40] They also incorporated the use of several books and added a "tuition free" summer term for the teachers as well.[41] In 1887, a new principal was appointed due to some squabbles that caused several teachers to resign.[42] During his years of service, John Cunningham changed the two year program to a three year program, with two years of study and one of professional practice, beginning in 1896.[43] In 1898, Robert Frazer took over.[44] The publication, *Normal Light*, records much of what happened in these years, but to sum it up Frazer saw to the tightening of admissions, to the repair and cleaning of the buildings, to the building of a gym, to the expansion of the library, and to issuing new books to students instead of forcing them to rent used ones.[45]

The date the original teaching labs closed is unknown, but we do know that the labs opened in 1970, according to the Virginia Department of Education.[46] These were in operation until 1982, with the nursery school remaining open until 2001. The school was for elementary through seventh and only served the children of faculty. The community's children could join if they won a lottery for open seats.[47] One of the adjuncts in the English Department at Longwood told me about going to school in this environment. She remembered her time there with fondness, and it must have indeed been a coveted public school environment.

Currently, the lab school idea has been reintroduced at Longwood University. However, they are partnering with Charlotte County Schools instead

38. Ibid.
39. Ibid., 56.
40. Ibid., 58.
41. Ibid.
42. Ibid., 64.
43. Ibid., 70.
44. Ibid., 80.
45. Ibid., 80, 85–86.
46. Division of Policy and Communications, "Lab Schools."
47. Ibid.

of the Prince Edward County Schools, even though Charlotte is a thirty to forty five minute drive from Farmville and the PECS schools are within a five minute drive from campus.[48] Using an $86,000 grant, Longwood will begin a summer lab school and then try to develop it into a year-round school later.[49] Instead of a lab school in Farmville, Longwood has begun offering a new one year M.A. program that puts experienced teachers in the public system in Farmville and Longwood students work in that system as "an extension of a lab school partnership" to benefit everyone involved.[50]

Conclusion

Most scholars note that teaching is still a profession largely occupied by women. As an acceptable form of employment in the nineteenth century, it allowed women to justify furthering their education as they made a living. It justified reaching higher and higher academically, eventually winning the right to an education equal to that offered to men. It subverted the very social paradigms meant to hold women in place by seeking to make them the very best occupants of that "place" or "sphere." Teaching, unlike any other profession, was extremely important in the rise for social equality for women since it gave women an opportunity to not just teach children, but to teach other adult women. It allowed them to open and lead in schools. It allowed them to vote on school matters. While teachers still make pathetically low wages (about $30K a year in Arizona), women could not have entered into other professions without showing a great deal of interest in this one.

Also, working as teachers and administrators in public schools gave them the opportunity to exercise their leadership skills. Again, women had the right to vote on school matters long before they won the right to vote for political candidates in the United States.[51]

Several First Ladies worked as teachers and several were later trained as teachers.

- Abigail Powers Filmore worked as a school teacher.

48. Longwood University, "Longwood Awarded."
49. Ibid..
50. Longwood University, "Longwood Offers."
51. Woody, *A History of Women's Education*, 1:441.

- Caroline Levinia Scott Harrison did so as well.[52] In fact, Caroline's father, a science and math professor, opened the Oxford Female Institute in Oxford, Ohio in 1849. "At the Institute, Caroline mastered English literature, for which she developed a life-long love, drama, music, art and painting. She graduated in 1853 with a degree in music. She taught music, home economics and painting, both in Oxford and in Kentucky."[53]

- Between 1882 and 1883, Helen Taft taught in a boys' school.

- Lou Henry Hoover was the first to attend a normal school. She went to San Jose Normal School from 1892 to 1893. After she earned her teaching certificate, she went to Stanford University from 1894 to 1898 and graduated with a B.A. in geology, making her the first woman in America to have ever earned this degree from this institution.[54]

While the idea of normal schools was one derived from the French, the idea that "teachers were born, not made," had to be overcome in the United States and great efforts had to go into creating curriculum for those who wanted to teach.[55] Institutions like Longwood University have a long history of working hard to prepare men and women for the classroom, and educators are kept on the cutting edge with requirements for updating their knowledge through required training and education each year. Today, education in America is characterized by politics, budget concerns, and "fill in the bubble testing," but it is always changing. In 2006, the Spellings Commission Report pushed all educational institutions into creating and implementing assessment cycles that made all institutions, both in K12 and college, more accountable. The Commission wrote:

> American higher education has been the envy of the world for years. In 1862, the First Morrill Act created an influential network of land-grant universities across the country. After World War II, the Serviceman's Readjustment Act of 1944, also known as the G.I. Bill made access to higher education a national priority. In the 1960s and 1970s, the launching and rapid growth of community colleges further expanded postsecondary educational

52. National First Ladies' Library, "First Ladies Research."

53. Ibid.

54. Ibid.

55. "Normal School." In *New World Encyclopedia*: http://www.newworldencyclopedia.org/entry/Normal_school.

opportunities. For a long time, we educated more people to higher levels than any other nation.[56]

However, they sought to prove the United States had fallen behind other countries in performance. Their findings alarmed our nation, and created the impetus for positive change. As the lower schools work to better prepare young men and women for college, and as institutions continue to take a long, hard look at themselves through data collected by assessments, we will continue to move toward a future of hope. Education will continue being a tool that helps to create and maintain the freedoms of its people. *All* of its people. As a representative case, Longwood University demonstrates just how much we still care about providing a high quality education for teachers and, in turn, to our students in public and private schools. It also demonstrates clearly the kinds of changes that many seminaries and academies underwent as they became normal schools, then colleges, and then, if they survived long enough, universities.

56. Spellings, "A Test of Leadership."

CONCLUSION

Alumni and Social Reform Movements

The Inspiration for Women's Involvement in Social Reform

SOCIAL REFORM MOVEMENTS SWEPT the United States in the nineteenth century and women not only participated in them but also played key leadership roles. During the early decades, temperance, abolition of slavery were important causes to which women were drawn, but by the end of century women's rights, especially suffrage, would be the central point of women's engagement in social reform.

A key source of the social reform movement was the Second Great Awakening. This revivalist movement (1790–1840) not only revitalized church attendance but also gave rise to a theological argument for Christians to engage in movements whose aim it was to improve conditions for the disenfranchised in American society. Charles Grandison Finney, a minister and revivalist, best articulated this religious rationale for social engagement. Significantly, Finney later served as the second president of Oberlin College, the first American institution of higher education to regularly admit women and African Americans.

The era in which Finney preached was dominated by a Christian world view known as "post-millennialism." According to this apocalyptic viewpoint, Christians would engage in building "the Kingdom of God on earth" in preparation for the return of Jesus Christ for his saints. Given the impact of the Industrial Revolution in developing and shaping both the positive and especially the negative aspects of urban America, it was obvious to most Christians that the United States was far from ready for Jesus' return. Within the confines of city tenements there was poverty, homelessness, orphans, drunkards, prostitutes, and if one looks to the rural South, there was the objectionable practice of human slavery. Female Christians of this time period not only witnessed these same social ills, but experienced their disenfranchisement in society, in the economy and in the church.

According to Finney, once converted, Christians were not only to preach repentance from sin as part of the Gospel message, but also engage in improving society. Thus both saving souls and social engagement served as a litmus test of one's Christian conversion. "Finney believed that regeneration resulted in radical moral transformation and that Christians should be actively involved in reforming all areas of their society."[1] This belief was based on Finney's view of benevolence which he saw as an outcome of the conversion. According to Finney, it was important for Christian to engage in social reform both for its intrinsic value and as a witness for the redemptive work of Jesus Christ. At the same time, according to Finney, it was important for Christians not to fixate on one particular reform or cause.

As the nineteenth century unfolded, these social reform movements would include the abolition of slavery, education reform, women's rights, women's suffrage, temperance and the treatment of the insane. Women would be key players in each of these movements.

Separate Spheres

However, as women engaged in social reform movements, the issue of "separate spheres" had to be addressed. From the first attempts at colonization of the land that came to be the United States to the initial phases of the Industrial Revolution, men and women tended to work side by side especially those in rural environs. As factories became the hub of economic enterprises, differentiation in spheres of work along gender lines started to become normative in the majority of industries. A result of this shift was a reinforcement of the concept of separate spheres for men and women.

> The gradual introduction and growth of factories, initially in the New England states, reflected a nation becoming more self-sufficient. The separation of home and wage work widened the gap between male and female duties, especially among the growing middle class. As more men took jobs in the public arena, female

1. Pak, "Social Reform," 104.

labor in the home became ever more important. Women engaged in hours of unpaid labor each day, cooking and baking, washing clothes, ironing, mending, cleaning lanterns, sewing clothes and linens, gardening, nursing the sick, and raising their children.[2]

There was now a growing separation into the "public" sphere for men and the "home" sphere for women. Instrumental in the idealization of domesticity as the sphere for women was not only the changing economic environment and reinforced social norms for the conduct of men and women, but also periodicals and newspapers that constituted budding mass media enterprises in the cities. The messaging in the articles, poems and novels authored by both men and women "exalted women's role in the home and glorified motherhood."[3] The literature of the era admonished women that their domestic work should be a fount of happiness and provided guidance to women regarding how to behave properly and carry out their work in the home.

Ironically one of the great proponents of this idealized domesticity was a woman, Catharine Beecher. Her book, *A Treatise on Domestic Economy, for the Use of Young Ladies at Home and at School*, is the first American complete guide to housekeeping. Written in 1841, although it begins with discussion of democracy and Christianity and woman's role in America, the bulk of the book achieves the hallmark of combining all facets of housekeeping into a single volume. By the time the book was written, Beecher was a proven educator, having founded Hartford Female Seminary in 1823 with the help of her sister. Still, she viewed women's position in society to be a subservient one, and she was opposed to women who abandoned their domestic duties in order to engage in expanded the roles of women in the public sphere.

Societal norms dovetailed well with religious beliefs of the time regarding the subservient role women were to serve in relation to their husbands. Utilizing a select set of verses from the Bible, many Christian leaders preached a message to women of obedience to their husbands and of their sacred duty within the home, raising her children and supporting her husband. Unfortunately, most Christian denominations barred women from roles in the "public" sphere of the church. The same was true outside the walls of the sanctuary—it was "unseemly" for a woman to speak in public regardless whether she was speaking to an audience of her own gender, or one which included both men and women. It is not surprising then, that

2. McMillen, *Seneca Falls*, 16–17.

3. Ibid., 17.

initial leadership in the women's movement comes from women raised as Quakers, as this Christian group did not march in lockstep with the Christian thinking of the time. Instead, Quakers had an egalitarian approach regarding gender including women having leadership roles in the church.

There were both societal and religious pressures for women, especially middle class women in the cities to live and conduct themselves according to prescribed roles. At the upper end of the economic spectrum, these women were to serve as "porcelain wives," the epitome of high society conduct. "Female submission was proclaimed to be part of God's order. In church, women were to sit in silence and never dream of occupying the pulpit. Numerous examples from scripture supported this, though as reformers like Lucretia Mott would later point out, just as many scriptural citations celebrated female strength and independence."[4]

There was great societal and religious pressures for women to both be subservient and keep themselves with the designated "home sphere." The media and literature of time with authors of both genders sought to reinforce these expectations of women. So, what was the impact of the literature and media message intended to bolster the concept of the idealized, domesticated American woman?

> One must ask whether the roles laid out in the prescriptive literature were intended to apply to all nineteenth century American women. And of course the answer is an emphatic no: The advice book were intended for an audience of middle and upper-middle class white northern urban women, at a time when a majority of Americans still lived on farms and the urban middle class was relatively small. Blacks and immigrant whites as well as all working class Americans were entirely excluded from the purview of the prescriptive literature. There is also an abundance of evidence to indicate that many nineteenth century women rejected these role models.[5]

The impetus for women engaging in the public sphere, both in speaking out against the social ills of their time but also taking on leadership roles in social reform movements has both secular and religious roots. As has been previously stated, an overarching religious influence for empowering women to engage in Christian and secular social reform was the rise of evangelicalism, a result of the second great awakening. Central to

4. Ibid., 18.
5. Norton, "The Paradox," 141.

evangelicalism was the belief that all individuals, male or female and regardless of color, were equally responsible to God. Since every person was a
sinner, each bore the responsibility for repentance and establishing a right
relationship with God. A second central tenet for evangelicals was the responsibility of each Christian to be "useful" to the kingdom of God. Given
the post-millennial paradigm of that time, and the great need to build the
kingdom of God in preparation for the return of Jesus Christ, there was
indeed enough work for everyone. Unfortunately, the positive impact of
this two-pronged belief primarily benefited white women.

The beginnings of the nineteenth century missionary and benevolence activity by women is quite evident. "Ministers encouraged female
volunteerism, especially in activities centered around the church such as
Bible study and prayer groups, maternal associations, and missionary organizations at home and abroad."[6] Women also organized various fundraising
activities in support of helping the destitute. Through the church, African
Americans in the Northeast organized literary and benevolence societies to
help the needy. Once such organization was the Colored Female Religious
and Moral Reform Society, founded in Salem, Massachusetts in 1818. The
intent of the organization was to provide mutual aid and self-help within
the African American community. Involvement in the CFRRMRS gave African American women a feeling of self-efficacy.

The Temperance Movement

One of the causes taken up in the early nineteenth century was temperance, which targeted the consumption of distilled liquor. The temperance
movement had special importance for women. Given how marriage was interpreted legally at the time, women's economic status was strongly aligned
to the man she married. If he was successful and a person of means, then
the woman would enjoy the benefits that accompanied her husband's level
of income. However, if her husband's life was negatively influenced by his
consumption of alcoholic beverages and he came to financial ruin, then the
woman's life would suffer as well. "Once a woman married, she forfeited
her legal existence. She couldn't sign a contract, make a will, or sue in a
court of law. If she received property from her father or other source, her
husband could sell it and keep the money for himself. He could apprentice
her children against her wishes, or assign them to a guardian of his own

6. McMillen, *Seneca Falls*, 43.

choosing. In the eyes of the law, explained the great legal authority Blackstone, 'the husband and the wife are one person,' and that person was the husband."[7] While there were religious motivations for women to become involved in the temperance movement, the parallel economic reasons were just as important.

The temperance movement was an interesting cross-section of interests between women, the clergy and business. In addition to the economic impact excessive drinking had on families, spousal abuse and physical beatings of the children were also outcomes. Regardless of the severity of the circumstances caused by a husband's drinking, women had little recourse because getting a divorce was so difficult in those days. Ministers were glad to take up the temperance cause as they would be contributing to establishing a virtuous society if he could get men on the righteous path of sobriety. The third of the influences was derived from capitalist interest. The business world was becoming more competitive economically, and employers were losing patience with workers who were late or missed work days because they were either drunk or hung over.

Temperance associations were founded as early as 1808 in New York and in 1813 in Massachusetts. The American Society for the Promotion of Temperance, an interdenominational effort, was founded by Presbyterian ministers Dr. Justin Edwards and Lyman Beecher, in 1826 in Boston. The movement went through an evolution to its target goal, from a reduction in the consumption of alcoholic beverages, to total abstinence, and finally to a ban on the manufacture and sale of alcohol. In addition to joining temperance societies, women signed pledges that they would never marry a man who drank and some made their prospective husbands sign "cold-water pledges" thus vowing never to consume alcoholic beverages.

As happened in the abolitionist movement, when women sought to participate in organizations founded by men, they were not allowed membership. The Sons of Temperance did not allow female members until 1853 and in that same year women were excluded from the World's Temperance Convention (WTC). Those members of the New York State Female Temperance Society were told to leave and return to their "proper sphere." In response, temperance leaders Lucy Stone, Susan B. Anthony, Antoinette Brown, William Garrison, Thomas Higginson, and others organized the first "Whole World's Temperance Convention."[8] They labeled the original

7. Gurko, *The Ladies of Seneca Falls*, 8.
8. McMillen, *Seneca Falls*, 56.

convention the "Half World Temperance Organization" because it excluded women. Over 2,000 people attended the gender-inclusive event held on September 23 and 24, 1853 in New York.

Through their involvement in the temperance movement women encountered very stark experiences with gender discrimination yet they labored on. They gained experience in signing and gathering petitions, organizing events, speaking in public. However, it was their involvement in the abolition movement that would heighten their awareness of their inferior status in American society to that point that they would launch a social reform movement which had a focus on women's rights.

The Abolition Movement

Thousands of women were involved in the movement to abolish slavery during the antebellum period. They formed anti-slavery associations such as the New England Female Anti-Slavery Society which was founded in 1831. When the male members of the American Anti-Slavery Society in Philadelphia did not invite women to join, a bi-racial group of women founded the Philadelphia Anti-Slavery Society in December, 1833. Such involvement was new to women as they were unaccustomed to organizing public gatherings, speaking in public, writing resolutions, circulating petitions and voting. "Above all, they learned to speak before an audience. It is difficult today to grasp the implication of this. In the early nineteenth century, women simply did not address a public group. It was considered not only beyond their capacities, but was frowned upon as improper, indecorous, unfeminine, irreligious, against both God and nature."[9] Women also wrote articles for abolitionist papers, circulated abolitionist pamphlets such as the Quakers' "The Appeal of the Religious Society of Friends in Pennsylvania, New Jersey, Delaware, etc., to their Fellow-Citizens of the United States on behalf of the Coloured Races," and "The Philosophy of the Abolition Movement" by Wendell Phillips. Women also circulated, signed, and delivered petitions to Congress calling for abolition. One such petition read in part:

> If these laws are ever to be repealed, and slavery and the slave trade in that District are thereby ever to cease, it must be by the action of Congress. Your petitioners believe that no time can be more favorable for such action than the present. They therefore most respectfully but earnestly entreat your honorable body to

9. Gurko, *The Ladies of Seneca Falls*, 35.

pass without such laws, as to your wisdom may seem right and proper for the entire abolition of slavery and the slave trade in the District of Columbia.[10]

Two of the very prominent women in the abolition movement were sisters Angelina and Sarah Grimke. Daughters of a prominent slave-holding family from South Carolina, these women saw firsthand the horrors of slavery and were very troubled. After the death of their father, Sarah moved to Philadelphia in 1821 and Angelina followed her north eight years later. Both sisters found affinity in the Quakers' core belief in human equality and became Quakers themselves. They joined the Philadelphia Anti-Slavery Society, where they met Lucretia Mott, a Quaker minister and ardent abolitionist.

Angelina's entry into the public debate regarding slavery was when in 1835, she sent a letter to famed abolitionist William Lloyd Garrison and he printed it in the Liberator, the anti-slavery paper Garrison published from 1831 to 1865. The following year, Angelina wrote, "An Appeal to the Christian Women of the South" in which she urged women of the South, "to pray, read, petition and persuade southern men of slavery's many evils."[11]

In 1836, the Grimke sisters were assigned by the American Anti-Slavery Society to spread the abolitionist message in "parlor talks," speaking to female audiences in New York and New Jersey. Initially these speaking engagements took place in individual homes but as audiences grew, the meetings were held in primarily in churches and sometimes in meeting halls. As would be a pattern in other reform movements of that era, men would soon join audiences that were intended to be for women only. Although both were effective speakers, of the two sisters, Angelina was the most eloquent and passionate in addressing audiences.

Sarah Grimke made her public entry with the publication of her "Epistle to the Clergy of the Southern States" in 1836. She took the very passages that southern ministers had used to justify slavery and demonstrated how they had misinterpreted Scripture. She pointed to the creation of men and women by God as evidence of equality of individuals and also questioned how any member of the clergy could sanction slavery. She urged ministers to remove the "sin" of slavery from the church.

In response to a gag rule passed by Congress in 1837 that tabled abolitionist petitions, over 100 black and white women assembled for the first meeting of the National Anti-Slavery Convention of American Women.

10. Moore Family Papers. ""Petition to the Congress."
11. McMillen, *Seneca Falls*, 60

Not only were these women challenging societal conventions about women's roles in the "public sphere," the biracial gathering also challenged societal rules about the division of the races. Women at the convention passed a resolution crafted by Angelina Grimke which challenged the societally prescribed roles for women which men rationalized with the use of biblical passages. According to Angelina, "It is the duty of woman, and the province of woman, to plead the cause of the oppressed in our land, and do all that she can by her voice, and her pen, and her purse, and the influence of her example, to overthrow the horrible system of American slavery."[12]

The Grimke sister's abolitionist work became a lightning rod for contention because they both engaged in the "public sphere" thought to be the domain of men, and they regularly addressed audiences that included both women and men. Although Angelina was the more prominent of the two sisters, it was Sarah who was "took the lead in defending women's rights. She was invited to write a series of letters on 'The Province of Woman' for the Spectator. These were reprinted in Garrison's Liberator and then published in book form as Letters on the Equality of the Sexes."[13]

Of all the opposition that females speaking in public like the Grimke's engendered, the strongest came from the clergy and from a female education reformer. "A Pastoral Letter of the General Association of Massachusetts to the Congregational Churches Under Their Care" was issued by the Massachusetts clergy and was to be read aloud in orthodox churches throughout Massachusetts. In the "Pastoral Letter," the clergy argued that women took on the role of public reformers, they were going against the teaching of the Bible which, according to the clergy's interpretation, limited women to subservient quiet roles of prayer and piety. Speaking in public like men did was "unnatural" an assault on women's "character."

Two "Clerical Appeals" followed the "Pastoral Letter," and these latter documents attacked Garrison's approach to abolition, which the clergy saw as to radical, as much as they attacked women abolitionists who spoke in public. These clerical missives had little effect on either Garrison or the Grimke sisters. In response to these attacks by the clergy, Angelina utilized an "equally created by God" argument and also argued that the female passivity and dependence emphasized in the "Pastoral Letter" was "not taught by the Bible . . . but was invented by man 'as a means to keep women in subjection.'"[14]

---

12. Ibid., 62.

13. Gurko, *Ladies of Seneca Falls*, 40.

14. Ibid., 41.

A critical event in the changing women's focus from anti-slavery activism to advocacy for women's rights was the World's Anti-Slavery Convention held in London, England in June, 1840. Several American antislavery societies send women as delegates to the convention. After traveling 3,000 miles, women found that they were barred from participating in the convention. Instead they were to sit silently as the men spoke. The only debate women were able to engage in were those at the boarding house where delegates were housed and the subject was women's right to participate in the convention and not slavery.

One delegate who experienced the blatant rejection from male co-laborers in the abolition movement was Lucretia Mott, a Quaker minister and a delegate to the convention from Philadelphia. "She bitterly regretted the split in the antislavery ranks, but with each new rebuff by the antislavery ranks, her resentment grew. The whole subject of women's rights began to assume new proportions until it became 'the most important question of my life.'"[15]

At the convention, Mott met Elizabeth Cady Stanton who was attending the event as the spouse of a delegate, her husband Henry Stanton. Elizabeth and Lucretia had shared beliefs regarding the abolition movement and the rights of women and the two soon became friends. Included in their discussion was possibly holding a women's rights convention. Little did they know at the time that they would both play critical roles in organizing just such an event which would become a milestone for the women's rights movement.

The Holiness Movement

According to the traditional historical narrative, the 1830s and 1840s are viewed as foundational decades for women's engagement in the social reform movements of the nineteenth century. A religious reform movement not normally included in this narrative was the holiness movement which was founded by women in the 1830s. This movement would not only influence the religious life of its adherents but would also significantly empower women to claim leadership roles not only in establishing churches and denominations but also educational enterprises from elementary schools to institutions of higher education.

The Holiness Movement followed the perfectionist impulse of John Wesley, and sought to restore piety to the Methodist Church which he had

15. Ibid., 55.

founded.[16] One of the outcomes of the First and Second Great Awakenings was the focus on living a sinless life, a perfectionist way of life. Central to achieving this sinless life was the experience of sanctification which meant a total surrender to God after the experience of salvation. Wesley tended to teach progressive sanctification, i.e., a number of gradual improvements until the individual could live the sinless life. Early adherents of the holiness movement believed that the experience of sanctification could be achieved instantaneously.

Individuals who had experienced this "instantaneous" sanctification found that it energized their faith walk. Female members of this nascent movement were provided with an avenue for sharing their experiences with the establishment of The Tuesday Meetings for the Promotion of Holiness by Sarah Lankford in 1835 in New York City. Lankford held these meetings in her home and when she moved away, her sister Phoebe Palmer took over the meetings in 1837 and articulated this newly found religious experience into what she called "altar theology." Central to Palmer's belief system was the experience of "sanctification," an experience in time during which a Christian surrendered one's heart to God and was able to live a life not controlled by sin. Instead of a continual improvement experience, according to Palmer's "shorter way," it could be a singular experience of total surrender to God. By 1839 Palmer was recognized as the leader of this new movement.

The significant contribution of the Tuesday Meetings to enabling women to have voice was that "public testimony" was a part of the Tuesday Meetings. Women would stand and share experiences from their walk of faith. The Tuesday Meetings became so popular that men asked to join and soon women were speaking in public to an audience of both women and men. This was quite scandalous at this juncture of American history. A second way in which women gained impetus for their public voice and leadership was the experience of sanctification itself. Having surrendered oneself totally to God and to his purposes for his or her life, it did not matter what society, culture, religion or the Christian church had to say, the individual was solely responsible to God. This was particularly significant for women who faced such opposition to public ministry.

Alma White, who would go on to found a church, a denomination, several elementary schools and Christian institutions of higher education, found in the experience of sanctification the ability to conquer the "man

16. Dieter, *The Holiness*, 22.

fearing spirit."[17] African American women who experienced sanctification also "experienced a conferral of personhood denied by larger social
constructions of African American and female subjectivity. For it is within
this divine dialogue that black women's subjectivity is produced even as
her agency is acknowledged and affirmed."[18] Through their experiences
of Christian conversion African American women claimed a sense of individual worth, and also found inspiration to fight against the system of
slavery. The experience of sanctification further empowered these wom-
en in their efforts of self-improvement for their own people and for the
betterment of society as a whole.

In his book, *Women and the Landscape of American Higher Education:
Wesleyan Holiness and Pentecostal Founders,*[19] Ruelas chronicles the intersection of expanded educational opportunities for women and their faith
experiences as they fulfilled faith-based careers and founded twenty-seven
Christian institutions of higher education in the United States. Depending
on whether the women were from the holiness movement, or the Pentecostal movement (which began at the outset of the twentieth century), the
personhood and calling of these women were confirmed by their religious
experiences. This empowered them to succeed in the midst of religious,
cultural and societal opposition to women operating freely as religious and
educational leaders in the "public sphere."

These women founders not only embraced their faith commitment
and educational training, but also the growing acceptance of teaching as
a socially accepted vocation for women. In addition to establishing evangelistic ministries, churches and denominations they also founded schools
across the educational spectrum from elementary schools to Bible institutes and Bible colleges. Significantly, even though historical accounts place
the beginning of the Bible institute movement in the 1880s to the establishment of Baptist Missionary School for women (1881), Nyack Missionary
College (1882) and Moody Bible Institute (1889), Eliza Garrett founded the
Garrett Bible Institute in 1853 (currently the Garrett-Evangelical Theological Seminary), almost thirty years before.[20]

Women in the holiness movement joined with their sisters from fellow Christian denominations to make cracks in the "stained glass ceiling"

17. Stanley, *Holy Boldness*, 211.
18. Ibid., 97.
19. Ruelas, *Women and the Landscape*.
20. Brereton, *Training God's Army*, 55; Moncher, "The Bible College," 106.

big enough so that one day access to the pulpit and participation in church leadership and polity would be truly egalitarian.

Seneca Falls and the Woman's Movement

Five women critical to the organization of the Woman's Rights Convention at Seneca Falls were Lucrieta Mott, Martha C. Wright, Mary Ann McClintock, Jane Hunt, and Elizabeth Cady Stanton. All but Stanton were Quakers and thus her journey to playing a crucial role in the history of women rights was made more difficult because she did not share the gender egalitarianism that her compatriots had experienced as members of the Quaker faith tradition.

Elizabeth Cady Stanton was the daughter of Judge Daniel and Margaret Cady. To her father's dismay three sons died in infancy and when his Eleazer died at the age of twenty, he said to Elizabeth, "Oh daughter, I wish you were a boy."[21] Elizabeth had always yearned for her father's approval and this declaration set her on a path of achievement "to be all my brother was."

Stanton attended the coeducational Johnstown Academy in Johnstown, New York and wanted to attend Union College, the school her brother was attending when he passed away. Unfortunately, neither Union nor any other United States college at the time was allowing admittance to women so she enrolled at the Troy Female Seminary in New York. Along with her academic work, Stanton attended the Christian revivals that were part of student life at Troy. Charles Finney preached at one of revivals Stanton attended and his preaching led to her skepticism regarding religion. The imagery he used regarding hell did not lead to repentance but to nightmares and states of depression and this solidified her skepticism about Christianity. Ironically, this same Finney who scared Elizabeth with his fire and brimstone sermons, served as an inspiration to Henry Stanton, Elizabeth's future husband, to become an abolitionist.

After much planning the Woman's Rights Convention was held on July 19 and 20, 1848 at Wesleyan Chapel in Seneca Falls, New York. The purpose of the convention was "to discuss the social, civil and religious condition and rights of woman."[22] Ironically, it was Lucretia's husband James who served as chairman of the convention because up until this time

---

21. Ward and Burns, *Not For Ourselves Alone*, 14.

22. Gurko, *Ladies of Seneca Falls*, 3.

a woman had not served as chairman of either abolition societies or events sponsored by these organizations.

In preparation for the convention, the five women organizers drafted a Declaration of Sentiments, a document intended to enumerate the rights of women. Although all five contributed to the crafting of the Declaration it was Stanton's decision to model it on Thomas Jefferson's Declaration of Independence. Although she had never addressed a public meeting before, it also fell to Stanton to present the Declaration at the Convention. The Declaration was approved by the convention's attendees and sixty-eight women affixed their signature to the document. Stanton then proposed eleven additional resolutions and ten passed without dissent. The eleventh had to do with women's suffrage, and although he had supported the Convention and the Declaration to this point, Stanton's husband Henry left the city because he did not want to be embarrassed by his wife's support of the suffrage resolution.

Things were at a standstill until ex-slave and abolition leader Frederick Douglass stood before the audience and spoke in favor of the eleventh resolution. His rationale was captured in text published in his paper, the *North Star*, a few days later: "All that distinguished man as an intelligent and accountable being is equally true of woman; and if that government only is just which governs by the free consent of the governed, there can be no reason in the world for denying to woman the exercise of the elective franchise, or a hand in making and administering the laws of the land. Our doctrine is that 'right is of no sex.'"[23]

Following Douglass' speech, a vote was taken, the eleventh resolution passed, and the Convention was adjourned. That first Woman's Rights Convention would serve as a launching point for the suffrage movement and the continuum of feminism in all of its prism-like variations. Women had seized upon all the educational opportunities afforded them, either through female seminaries or sectarian schools and had been prepared for this moment of truth.

The Occupational Ripple Effect

In the aftermath of slavery, the only "white collar" job to which an African American man could aspire, especially in the South, was that of minister. With the advent of the Civil Rights movement, the main core of the

23. Ward and Burns, *Not For Ourselves Alone*, 41.

intelligentsia and leadership came from African American clergymen. Similarly, the first societally acceptable occupation for women was that of teacher. Whether as educators with secular aspirations of expanding educational opportunities within society or persons of faith who were answering God's call upon their lives, founding schools became almost a natural outcome of women's endeavors. In addition to educating women who would engage social reform movements of the nineteenth century, female seminaries provided women with the knowledge and skill set to found schools across the educational spectrum.

The contributions of those who founded, fought for, and taught at the female seminaries and academies in the United States cannot be overstated when put into the context of how women began to obtain social justice in this country. While the history of these institutions is a complex history and while it is still underexplored, it is vital to understand that women's rights did not evolve out of a simple rejection of Christianity or out of hatred for men. The social justice obtained by women was an outgrowth of their education, with education feeding into social changes that could not be stemmed once begun. These early institutions boldly proclaimed a desire to propagate Christianity and Christian values and these were not viewed as limitations that had to be endured, but as heartfelt goals for missionary-teachers. Although it is not a simple history, it is our hope that we have helped twenty-first-century readers better understand the truth of how women worked toward empowerment in the United States.

Bibliography

"Academies and Seminaries." Women's Education Evolves, 1790–1890. University of Michigan, 2005. Online: http://www.clements.umich.edu/exhibits/online/womened/index.html.

Adams, Abigail. "Letter from Abigail Adams to John Adams, August 14, 1776." *History Tools*. Online: www.historytools.org/sources/Abigail-John-Letters.pdf.

Agnew, Brad. "Seminary Hall Narrative: 1846–2014." Northeastern State University, Seminary Hall. 2014. Online: http://offices.nsuok.edu/seminaryhall/SeminaryHallNarrativebyDrBradAgnew.aspx.

"Alice M. Robertson." McFarlin Library, University of Tulsa. Online: http://www.lib.utulsa.edu/digital/robertson/Series_III/pdf/AR3_01_02_28.pdf.

Anderson, James D. *The Education of Blacks in the South, 1860–1935*. Chapel Hill: University of North Carolina Press, 1988.

Andrews, William L., ed. *Sisters of the Spirit: Three Black Women's Autobiographies of the Nineteenth Century*. Bloomington: Indiana University Press, 1986.

Baker, Jean H. *Mary Todd Lincoln: A Biography*. New York: Norton, 1987.

Beecher, Catharine E. "An Essay on the Education of Female Teachers, Written at the Request of the American Lyceum." Microfilm, 2–22. New York: Van Nostrand and Dwight, 1835.

Berkin, Carol Ruth, and Mary Beth Norton, eds. *Women of America: A History*. Boston: Houghton Mifflin, 1979.

Berry, Wendell. "The Peace of Wild Things." In *Risking Everything: 110 Poems of Love and Revelation*, edited by Roger Housden, 102. New York: Harmony, 2003.

Bizzell, Patricia, and Bruce Herzberg. "Christine de Pizan." In *The Rhetorical Tradition: Readings from the Classical Times to the Present*, 540–43. 2nd ed. Boston: Bedford/St. Martin's, 2001.

———. "Margaret Fell." In *The Rhetorical Tradition: Readings from the Classical Times to the Present*, 748–52. 2nd ed. Boston: Bedford/St. Martin's, 2001.

Bradford, M.E. "The Older Rhetoric Revisited: Hugh Blair and the Public Virtue of Style." Online: http://www.kirkcenter.org/index.php/bookman/article/older-rhetoric-revisited-hugh-blair/.

Brekus, Catherine. *Strangers and Pilgrims: Female Preaching in America, 1740–1845*. Chapel Hill: University of North Carolina Press, 1998.

Bibliography

Brereton, Virginia Lieson. *Training God's Army: The American Bible School, 1880–1940.* Bloomington: Indiana University Press, 1990.

Butchart, Ronald E. *Schooling the Freed People: Teaching, Learning and the Struggle for Black Freedom, 1861–1876.* Chapel Hill: University of North Carolina Press, 2010.

Carney, Cary Michael. *Native American Higher Education in the United States.* New Brunswick, NJ: Transaction, 1999.

Carr, S. J. "Bloomfield Academy and Its Founder." *The Chronicles of Oklahoma* 2/4 (December 1924) 366–79.

Cauchi, Tony, "Lucy F. Farrow." Revival Library. 2004. Online: http://www.revival-library. org/pensketches/am_pentecostals/farrow.html.

Clinton, Catherine, "Equally Their Due: The Education of the Planter Daughter in the Early Republic." In *History of Women's Education in the United States: Historical Articles on Women's Lives and Activities,* edited by Nancy Cott, 12:3–24. Munich: K.G. Saur, 1993.

Cobb, Amanda. *Listening to our Grandmother's Stories: The Bloomfield Academy for Chickasaw Females, 1852–1949.* Lincoln: University of Nebraska Press, 2002.

Colby, Catherine. "Wheelock Academy: Model for the Indian Territory." *Cultural Resource Management* 20/9 (1997) n.p. Online: http://crm.cr.nps.gov/archive/20-9/20-9-14.pdf.

Collier-Thomas, Bettye. "The Impact of Black Women in Education: An Historical Overview." *The Journal of Negro Education* 51/3 (Summer 1982) 173–80.

———. *Jesus, Jobs, and Justice: African American Women and Religion.* New York: Knopf, 2010.

"Colonial Heritage: Boarding Schools." National First Ladies' Library, 2013. Online: http://www.firstladies.org/biographies/.

Cott, Nancy F. *No Small Courage: A History of Women in the United States.* Oxford: Oxford University Press, 2000.

Davison, Oscar William. "Oklahoma's Educational Heritage." *Chronicles of Oklahoma* 27/4 (Winter 1949–50) 354–72. http://digital.library.okstate.edu/chronicles/v027/v027p354.pdf.

de la Cruz, Sor Juana Ines. "From The Poet's Answer to the Most Illustrious Sister Filotea de la Cruz." In *The Rhetorical Tradition: Readings from Classical Times to the Present,* edited by Patricia Bizzell and Bruce Herzberg, 780–88. 2nd ed. Boston: Bedford/St. Martin's, 2001.

de Pizan, Christine. "From The Book of the City of Ladies." In *The Rhetorical Tradition: Readings from the Classical Times to the Present,* edited by Patricia Bizzell and Bruce Herzberg, 544–45. 2nd ed. Boston: Bedford/St. Martin's, 2001.

Dieter, Melvin E. *The Holiness Revival of the Nineteenth Century.* 2nd ed. Lanham, MD: Scarecrow, 1996.

Division of Policy and Communications. "Lab Schools." Virginia Department of Education, 2010. Online: www.doe.virginia.gov/.../schools/.../lab_schools_presentation.ppt.

Domenico, Roy P., and Mark Y. Hanley, eds. *Encyclopedia of Modern Christian Politics.* Westport, CT: Greenwood, 2006.

Dunham, Elizabeth. "The Choctaw People in the Southeast." Special Collections Library, 2006. Online: http://www.lib.utk.edu/special/guides/choctaw.pdf.

Durham, Joseph T. "The Other Side of the Story: The World of African-American Academies in the South After the Civil War." *The Negro Educational Review* 54/1–2 (January–April 2003) 3–16.

Educational Policy Institute. "The Landscape of Public Education: A Statistical Portrait Throughout the Years." *EpicCenter* (April 2011) n.p. Online: http://www. educationalpolicy.org/publications/EPI%20Center/EPICenter_K-12-CUT.pdf.

Eisenmann, Linda, ed. *Historical Dictionary of Women's Education in the United States.* Westport, CT: Greenwood, 1998.

Ellis, Clyde. "American Indians and Education." *Encyclopedia of Oklahoma History and Culture.* Online: http://digital.library.okstate.edu/encyclopedia/entries/a/am012. html.

Emerson, Ralph Waldo. "1836 Letter to President Van Buren." Cherokee Nation, 2014. Online: http://www.cherokee.org/AboutTheNation/History/TrailofTears/ RalphWaldoEmersonsLetter.aspx.

"Farmville Female College, Home School for Young Ladies." Brochure at Longwood University Library. Baltimore: John W. Woods, 1859.

Faulk, Odie B., and William D. Welge. *Oklahoma: A Rich Heritage.* Sun Valley, CA: American Historical, 2004.

Fell, Margaret. "Women's Speaking Justified, Proved, and Allowed by the Scriptures." In *The Rhetorical Tradition: Readings from the Classical Times to the Present,* edited by Patricia Bizzell and Bruce Herzberg, 753–60. 2nd ed. Boston: Bedford/St. Martin's, 2001.

Foreman, Carolyn Thomas. "The Choctaw Academy." *The Chronicles of Oklahoma* 6/4 (December 1928) 453–79. Online: http://digital.library.okstate.edu/Chronicles/ v006/v006p453.html.

Foster, Hannah Webster. *The Boarding School: Or, Lessons of a Preceptress to Her Pupils; Consisting of Information, Instruction, and Advice, Calculated to Improve the Manners, and Form the Character of Young Ladies. To which is Added, a Collection of Letters, Written by the Pupils, to Their Instructress, Their Friends, and Each Other.* Boston: Peaslee, 1829. Online: http://books.google.com/books/about/The_Boarding_School. html?id=emN1eV46dkIC.

"The Fourth Annual Catalogue of Farmville College, Farmville, Prince Edward County, Virginia." Longwood University Library. Baltimore: Charles Harvey Co., 1876–77.

Frank, Andrew K. "Seminole." *Encyclopedia of Oklahoma History and Culture* (2007). Online: http://digital.library.okstate.edu/encyclopedia/entries/s/se011.html.

Fraser, James W. *Preparing America's Teachers: A History.* New York: Teacher's College Press, 2007.

Geiger, Roger, ed. *History of Higher Education Annual* 22 (2002).

Goodsell, Willystine. *Pioneers of Women's Education in the United States: Emma Willard, Catharine Beecher, Mary Lyon.* New York: Amis, 1970.

Gurko, Miriam. *The Ladies of Seneca Falls: The Birth of the Woman's Right Movement.* New York: Schocken, 1974.

Guy-Sheftall, Beverly. "Black Women and Higher Education: Spelman and Bennett Colleges Revisited." *Journal of Negro Education* 51/3 (1982) 278–87.

Hampden-Sydney College. "About H-SC." Online: http://www.hsc.edu/About-H-SC/ History-of-H-SC.html.

Heyrman, Christine Leigh, "The First Great Awakening." National Humanities Center, 2014. Online: http://nationalhumanitiescenter.org/tserve/eighteen/ekeyinfo/ grawaken.htm.

Higginbotham, Evelyn Brooks. *Righteous Discontent: The Women's Movement in the Black Baptist Church, 1880–1920.* Cambridge, MA: Harvard University Press, 1993.

BIBLIOGRAPHY

"Horace Mann." *Bio*, 2013. Online: http://www.biography.com/people/horace-mann-9397522.

"Horace Mann (1796–1859)." Only a Teacher: Schoolhouse Pioneers. *PBS*. Online: http://www.pbs.org/onlyateacher/horace.html.

Horowitz, Helen. *Alma Mater: Design and Experience in the Women's Colleges from Their Nineteenth-Century Beginnings to the 1930s*. New York: Knopf, 1984.

Jordan, James. "Once Upon a Time in the Rotunda: The Presence of the Past." *Longwood: A Magazine for the Alumni and Friends of Longwood College* 2/2 (2001). Online: http://www.longwood.edu/longwood/Summer01/firerotunda.html.

Koenig, Pamela. "Seminole Schools." *Encyclopedia of Oklahoma History and Culture* (2007). Online: http://digital.library.okstate.edu/encyclopedia/entries/S/SE013.html.

Lerner, Gerda, ed. *Black Women in White America: A Documentary History*. New York: Vintage, 1972.

Lincoln, C. Eric, and Lawrence H. Mamiya. *The Black Church in the African American Experience*. Durham, NC: Duke University Press, 1990.

Lindley, Susan Hill. *You Have Stept out of Your Place: A History of Women and Religion In America*. Louisville: John Knox, 1996.

Lindman, Janet Moore. "Beyond the Meetinghouse: Women and Protestant Spirituality in Early America." In *The Religious History of American Women: Reimagining the Past*, edited by Catherine Brekus, 142–60. Chapel Hill: University of North Carolina Press, 2007.

Litchfield Historical Society. "A History of the Litchfield Female Academy." 2013.Online: http://www.litchfieldhistoricalsociety.org/history/academy.php.

Longwood University. "Award Descriptions." Online: http://www.longwood.edu/leadership/13197.htm.

———. "Joan of Arc Leadership Program." Online: http://www.longwood.edu/leadership/13137.htm.

———. "Longwood Awarded Planning Grant to Establish Laboratory School." May 10, 2012. Online: http://www.longwood.edu/2012releases_42916.htm.

———. "Longwood Offers New One-Year Master's in Elementary Education." January 18, 2013. Online: http://www.longwood.edu/2013releases_46176.htm.

Lowenberg, Bert James, and Ruth Bogin, eds. *Black Women in Nineteenth-Century American Life*. University Park: Pennsylvania State University Press, 1976.

Lyon, Mary. "The Inception of Mount Holyoke College; Portions of Letters Written by Mary Lyon between 1831 and 1837." Springfield, MA: Springfield Printing and Binding, n.d.

Martina, Sylvia L. M. "Emma Hart Willard." In *Encyclopedia of Educational Reform and Dissent*, edited by T. Hunt et al., 1:943. Thousand Oaks, CA: Sage, 2010.

McCullagh, James. "The Closing of the Female Cherokee Seminary in 1857: Remembering the 'Rosebuds.'" *The Goingsnake Messenger* 23/3 (2006) 50–58.

———. "Eliza Jane Ross: A Cherokee Pioneer Educator." *The Chronicles of Oklahoma* 87 (Summer 2009) 224–43.

———. "Mayme Jane Starr (1879–1901): A 'Cherokee Rose Bud' and Her Family Remembered." *The Chronicles of Oklahoma* 110 (Winter 2012–13) 477–91.

———. *The Teachers of the Cherokee Nation Public Schools: 1870s–1907*. Tahlequah, OK: Cherokee Heritage, 2012.

Bibliography

McMillen, Sally G. *Seneca Falls and the Origins of the Women's Rights Movement.* Oxford: Oxford University Press, 2008.

Melder, Keith. "Mask of Oppression: The Female Seminary Movement in the United States." In *History of Women's Education in the United States: Historical Articles on Women's Lives and Activities,* edited by Nancy Cott. 12:25–44. Munich: K.G. Saur, 1993.

Mihesuah, Devon. *Cultivating the Rosebuds: The Education of Women at the Cherokee Female Seminary, 1851–1909.* Urbana: University of Illinois Press, 1993.

Miles, Dennis B. "Choctaw Boarding Schools." *Encyclopedia of Oklahoma History and Culture.* Online: *digital.library.okstate.edu/encyclopedia/entries/C/CH049.html.*

"The Missionary Impulse." *Digital History* (2013). Online: http://www.digitalhistory.uh.edu/disp_textbook.cfm?smtid=3&psid=683.

Momaday, N. Scott. "The Delight Song of Tsaoi-talee." The Poetry Foundation. Online: http://www.poetryfoundation.org/poem/175895.

Moncher, Gary. "The Bible College and American Moral Culture." PhD diss., University of California at Berkeley, 1987.

Moore Family Papers. "Petition to the Congress of the United States." Unpublished. Old Sturbridge Village Research Library, 1835.

Moore, Hannah Milcah Hill. *Miscellanies, Moral and Instructive, in Prose and Verse; Collected from Various Authors, for the Use of Schools, and Improvement of Young Persons of Both Sexes.* 1796.

Moravian College. "College History." 2013. Online: http://www.moravian.edu/default.aspx?pageid=37.

More, Hannah, "Chapter 1: An Address to Women of Rank and Fortune." In *Women's Worlds: The McGraw-Hill Anthology of Women's Writing,* edited by Robyn Warhol-Down et al., 296–306. Boston: McGraw-Hill, 2008.

Moss, Hilary J. *Schooling Citizens: The Struggle for African American Education in Antebellum America.* Chicago: University of Chicago Press, 2009.

Nash, Margaret A. *Women's Education in the United States, 1780–1840.* New York: Palgrave McMillan, 2005.

National First Ladies' Library. "First Ladies Research." Online: http://www.firstladies.org/biographies/.

National Women's History Museum. "Women's Changing Roles as Citizens of a New Republic: 1700's." 2014. Online: https://www.nwhm.org/online-exhibits/education/1700s_2.htm.

Noll, Mark A. *America's God: From Jonathan Edwards to Abraham Lincoln.* Oxford: Oxford University Press, 2002.

Norton, Mary Beth. *Liberty's Daughters: The Revolutionary Experience of American Women, 1750–1800.* Ithaca, NY: Cornell University Press, 1980.

———. "The Paradox of 'Women's Sphere.'" In *Women of America: A History,* edited by Carol Ruth Berkin and Mary Beth Norton, 139–49. Boston: Houghton Mifflin, 1979.

"One Hundredth Anniversary of the Opening of the Cherokee National Seminaries: 1851–1951." Microfilm. Northeastern State University. May 7, 1951.

The Oxford English Study Bible: Revised English Bible with the Apocrypha. Edited by M. Jack Suggs, Katharine Doob Sakenfeld, and James R. Meuller. New York: Oxford University Press, 1992.

Pak, Ung-Kyu. "Social Reform and Theology in the Ministry of Charles G. Finney." *Theological Forum* 58 (2009) 101–39.

Raboteau, Albert J. *A Fire in the Bones: Reflections on African-American Religious History.* Boston: Beacon, 1995.

———. *Slave Religion: The "Invisible Institution" in the Antebellum South.* Oxford: Oxford University Press, 2004.

Read, Florence M. *The Story of Spelman College.* Princeton, NJ: Princeton University Press, 1961.

Reid, Ronald Forest. *Edward Everett: Unionist Orator.* Westport, CT: Greenwood, 1990.

Reid, Yolanda, and Rick Gregory. *Robertson County, Tennessee: Home of the World's Finest, Celebrating 200 Years.* Paducah, KY: Turner, 1996.

"Religion, Race, and Culture; Religion in Schools." University of Michigan, 2005. Online: http://www.clements.umich.edu/exhibits/online/womened/Religion.html.

Robertson, Stephen L. "Biographies of the First Ladies." In *The Presidents, First Ladies, and Vice Presidents: White House Biographies, 1789–2005,* edited by Daniel C. Diller and Stephen L. Robertson, 145–204. Washington, DC: CQ, 2005.

Ruelas, Abraham. *Women and the Landscape of American Higher Education: Wesleyan Holiness and Pentecostal Founders.* Eugene, OR: Wipf & Stock, 2010.

Rush, Benjamin. "Thoughts Upon Female Education." Boston, 1787. Online: http://www.swarthmore.edu/SocSci/rbannis1/AIH19th/female.html.

Scott, Donald. "Evangelicalism, Revivalism, and the Second Great Awakening." National Humanities Center, 2000. Online: http://nationalhumanitiescenter.org/tserve/nineteen/nkeyinfo/nevanrev.htm.

Sernett, Milton C., ed. *African-American Religious History: Documentary Witness.* 2nd ed. Durham, NC: Duke University Press, 1999.

Slowe, Lucy D. "Higher Education of Negro Women." *The Journal of Negro Education* 2/3 (July 1933) 352–58.

Smith-Rosenberg, Carroll. *Religion and the Rise of the American City: The New York City Mission Movement, 1812–1870.* Ithaca, NY: Cornell University Press, 1971.

Spellings, Margaret. "A Test of Leadership: Charting the Future of American Higher Education." U. S. Department of Education, 2006. Online: http://www2.ed.gov/about/bdscomm/list/hiedfuture/reports/final-report.pdf.

Sprague, Rosemary. *Longwood College: A History.* Richmond, VA: William Byrd, 1989.

Stanley, Susie. *Holy Boldness: Women Preachers' Autobiographies and the Sanctified Self.* Knoxville: University of Tennessee Press, 2002.

Starr, Emmet. *History of the Cherokee Indians.* Cherokee, NC: Cherokee, 2009.

Staude, Ryan. "The Cornerstone of the Republic: George Washington and the National University." In *Inequity in Education: A Historical Perspective,* edited by Debra Meyers and Burke Miller, 35–54. Lanham, MD: Rowman & Littlefield, 2009.

Sutherland, Christine Mason. "Mary Astell: Reclaiming Rhetorica in the Seventeenth Century." *Reclaiming Rhetorica: Women in the Rhetorical Tradition,* edited by Andrea A. Lunsford, 93–116. Pittsburg: University of Pittsburgh Press, 1995.

Sweet, Leonard. "The Female Seminary Movement and Woman's Mission in Antebellum America." *Church History* 54/1 (March 1985) 41–55.

Synan, Vinson. *The Century of the Holy Spirit: 100 Years of Pentecostal and Charismatic Renewal 1901–2001.* Nashville: Thomas Nelson, 2001.

Tomaselli, Sylvana. "Mary Wollstonecraft." *The Stanford Encyclopedia of Philosophy* (Summer 2014). Online: http://plato.stanford.edu/archives/sum2014/entries/wollstonecraft/.

BIBLIOGRAPHY

Trevathan, Robert E. "School Days at Emahaka Academy." *The Chronicles of Oklahoma* 38 (Autumn 1960) 265–73. Online: http://digital.library.okstate.edu/Chronicles/vo38/vo38p265.pdf.

Tucker, Ruth A., and Walter Liefeld. *Daughters of the Church: Women and Ministry from New Testament Times to the Present.* Grand Rapids: Zondervan, 1987.

University Archives and Records Center. "The Charity School: Overview." University of Pennsylvania, 2004. Online: http://www.archives.upenn.edu/histy/features/1700s/charitysch.html.

Vaughn, Betty Huddleston. "Douglas H. C. Johnston." N.d. Online: http://vidas.rootsweb.ancestry.com/soo4.html.

Volo, James M., and Dorothy Denneen Volo. *Family Life in 17th and 18th Century America.* Westport, CT: Greenwood, 2006.

Wakefield, Priscilla. *Mental Improvement: Or the Beauties and Wonders of Nature and Art in a Series of Instructive Conversations.* New Bedford, MA: Abraham Shearman, 1799.

Ward, Geoffrey C., and Ken Burns. *Not For Ourselves Alone: The Story of Elizabeth Cady Stanton and Susan B. Anthony.* New York: Knopf, 1999.

Watson, Robert. *American First Ladies.* Pasadena, CA: Salem, 2002.

Welch, Kristen Dayle. *Women with the Good News: The Rhetorical Heritage of Pentecostal Holiness Women Preachers.* Cleveland, TN: Centre for Pentecostal Theology, 2010.

White, Deborah Gray. *Ar'n't I a Woman? Female Slaves in the Plantation South.* New York: Norton, 1999.

The White House. "Our First Ladies: Sarah Polk." Online: http://www.whitehouse.gov/about/first-ladies/sarahpolk.

Willard, Emma. "An Address to the Public, Particularly to the Members of the Legislature of New York, Proposing a Plan for Improving Female Education." Middlebury, VT: J. W. Copeland, 1819.

Williams, Juan, and Quinton Dixie. *This Far by Faith.* New York: HarperCollins, 2003.

Wollstonecraft, Mary. *Thoughts on the Education of Daughters, With Reflections on Female Conduct in the More Important Duties of Life.* London: J. Johnson, 1787. Online: https://archive.org/details/thoughtsoneducaoounkngoog.

———. *A Vindication of the Rights of Woman.* Eugene: University of Oregon, 2000. Online: https://scholarsbank.uoregon.edu/xmlui/bitstream/handle/1794/785/vindication.pdf.

Woodson, Carter G. *The Mis-Education of the Negro.* Mineola, NY: Dover, 2005.

Woody, Thomas. *A History of Women's Education in the United States.* 2 vols. New York: Octagon, 1966.

Wright, James. "A Blessing." In *Risking Everything: 110 Poems of Love and Revelation,* edited by Roger Housden, 69. New York: Harmony, 2003.

Wyman, Andrea. "The Earliest Early Childhood Teachers: Women Teachers of America's Dame Schools." *Young Children* 50/2 (January 1995) 29–32.

"Young Ladies' Seminary, Benicia. Catalogue for the Fifth Year ending May, 1957." San Francisco: Whitton, Towne, 1957.

Zondervan NIV Study Bible. Edited by Kenneth L. Barker. Grand Rapids: Zondervan, 2008.

www.ingramcontent.com/pod-product-compliance
Lightning Source LLC
Chambersburg PA
CBHW071100280326
41928CB00050B/2573